THE BEST OF MIXED MARTIAL ARTS

presented by MMA Worldwide and TapouT
with Randy Couture

TRIUMPH
BOOKS

THE BEST OF MIXED MARTIAL ARTS

Library of Congress Control Number: 2007907046

This book is available in quantity at special discounts for your group or organization. For further information, contact:

Triumph Books
542 South Dearborn Street
Suite 750
Chicago, Illinois 60605
(312) 939-3330
Fax (312) 663-3557

Printed in USA
ISBN: 978-1-60078-088-2
Design by MMA Worldwide, Inc.
Photo credits by MMA Worldwide, Inc.

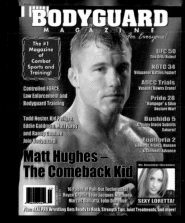

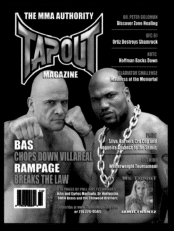

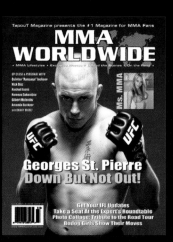
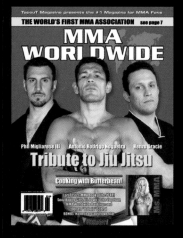

We are very proud to bring you this special collection of what has made *TapouT & MMA Worldwide Magazines* the best in the business. Always evolving, we knew it took a unique balance of instructionals, fighter profiles, health/conditioning articles and event pages to meet the demands of our fans. With the Internet, other MMA magazines and now the mainstream press, *our magazines* have been able to carve their own niche to provide the reader with something they can't get anywhere else. And being in the publishing business for over a decade, we knew that fans of the fastest growing sport deserved the best quality in the industry.

Over these 112 pages, you'll find some of our best instructional pages from the greatest fighters and trainers in the world, including: Royce Gracie, Quinton Jackson, Bas Rutten, Matt Hughes, Ken Shamrock and Antonio Rodrigo Nogueira.

Many of you are not in my backyard, Southern California—the Mecca of MMA, so I'm happy to bring you the knowledge these mixed martial arts masters have to offer. In addition, you'll find conditioning pages from Randy Couture, Eddie Bravo and Zach Even-Esch just to name a few.

We have published stories on the sport's biggest names, so it took us some time to narrow a "best of" for this collection. You'll find stories on Randy Couture, Quinton Jackson, Chuck Liddell, B J Penn, Antonio Nogueira, Georges St. Pierre, Dan Henderson, Royce Gracie, and Matt Hughes just to get you started. The mental and physical fortitude these ultimate athletes possess is an inspiration to us all.

Coming to a city near you!

When I started *Bodyguard Magazine*, I had no idea what I was getting myself into. As a life-long martial artist, it was something close to my heart, but I had no idea just how well it would take off. Since changing our name to *TapouT Magazine*, we have since created another magazine, *MMA Worldwide*, a radio show and an upcoming reality TV show. I've been in sales all my life, but the easiest sale for me is creating more value for the fan and making it easier for him/her to stay connected to this incredible sport.

I hope you like *The Best of TapouT & MMA Worldwide Magazine* and will continue to buy us off the newsstands or subscribe to us because we are here to stay!

Robert "The Closer" Pittman

Contents

BODYGUARD • TAPOUT • MMA WORLDWI

Mixed Martial Arts Promotions:
Past, Present and Future

by **Bobby Pittman**

Mixed martial arts isn't anything new. It was the third combative sport added to the original Greek Olympics as a way to find the best wrestler amongst boxers and the best boxer amongst wrestlers. As far back as 648 B.C., the sport was called pankration. Pankrationists were viewed as the greatest athletes in those early Olympic games, and in one form or another, the sport has flourished ever since. Practiced all over the world, it has been called catch wrestling, shoot fighting, vale tudo, no-holds-barred fighting, freestyle fighting and much more. The Ultimate Fighting Championship wasn't even created as a sport in November 1993 and struggled for years to claim the proper name for a sport, which became mixed martial arts or MMA. Since then MMA promoters have strived to create a mainstream sport with a commonality of rules, regulations and weight classes. Many promoters have jumped onboard and it seems there are new promotions popping up every day. Here is a brief look at the MMA promotions that helped shape the athletes and the sport as we know it today.

ULTIMATE FIGHTING CHAMPIONSHIP (UFC)

This is the "Grand Daddy" of them all. Although certain events in other countries may have preceded the UFC, this is now the world's leading promotion, playing host to the world's greatest fighters. Brazilian jiu-jitsu master Rorion Gracie, ad man Art Davie and SEG programming director Campbell McLaren are the trio responsible for creating the UFC with the basic premise of pitting martial artists of different styles against one another to see whose style was truly the best. These early events became a pay-per-view bonanza, but the spectacle over sport approach created a political firestorm. Politicians led by John McCain desperately wanted this new "human cockfighting" shut down. After their fifth event, Gracie and Davie sold their interest in the franchise to SEG. Davie continued with SEG to promote their events, but the pressure from authorities to ban the sport made it very difficult for the new company. Eventually they were dropped from cable companies after UFC XII and found their success rapidly decreasing, which brought them into what some early fans have dubbed the "dark ages."

In an effort to avoid bankruptcy, SEG President Robert Meyrowitz attempted to gain sanctioning and get back on pay-per-view. Running out of money, however, the promotion was sold to Las Vegas moguls Lorenzo and Frank Fertitta in 2001. Since then, under the guidance of Zuffa President Dana White, the UFC has grown into what it is today: the leading MMA promotion of the fastest growing sport in the world. They have succeeded in getting the sport sanctioned in Las Vegas, where they host the majority of their sold-out events. The shows are now featured on PPV, Spike TV and even covered in the mainstream media. The UFC and MMA go hand in hand for fans, but a sport is made up of more than one promotion.

PRIDE FIGHTING CHAMPIONSHIPS

Pride was the world's best promotion of their time. At one point, they had the best fighters and constantly put on stellar shows. With their inaugural show held at the Tokyo Dome in Japan and over 60 shows that followed, Pride set the all-time attendance record for an MMA event with a reported 70,000 paid at the Pride/K-1 co-promotion, Shockwave. Even with the huge following that Pride had gained, controversy surrounded the company, as some believed Pride was a front for the yakuza or Japanese mafia. As time went on, the promotion lost its deal with Fuji TV and was never able to regain its status as a major player. Ultimately, they were forced to sell to the UFC who, despite previously stating they had plans to continue promoting shows, didn't do much with the company, save for cherry-picking their stars. Pride Fighting Championships may be gone, but early fans will remember some of the most incredible matches to ever take place in the sport.

RINGS FIGHTING NETWORK

Rings is one of the most misunderstood events in MMA history. Started by Akira Maeda, a popular shoot wrestler, the colorful international event known as Rings Fighting Network hosted an incredible stable of international talent beginning in 1991. Thing is, most of the matches that took place in Rings had predetermined endings, save for their shows outside of Japan. That all changed in 1999 when Rings, in an effort to compete against the UFC and Pride, modified its promotion to include fighting with four-ounce gloves (instead of open hands), new MMA rules (old rules mimicked stiff-worked pro wrestling matches with rope escapes), and most importantly, no more worked matches. Rings is the only MMA promotion to run shows in more countries than anywhere else, including Holland, Australia, Russia, Georgia, Lithuania, Ireland and the United States. With two major 32-man tournaments that took place, some of the sport's most popular stars got their shot in the big time with Rings. Fedor Emelianenko, Ricardo Arona, Rodrigo "Minotauro" Nogueira and many others were seen regularly in the promotion. Unfortunately it didn't last long and Rings ended up falling apart with their fighters left to fend for themselves. While many of them moved to Pride, the promotion that made them stars will never be forgotten.

SHOOTO

Although Shooto has never gained mainstream popularity, it should be mentioned here simply for being early pioneers of MMA. Shooto was formed in 1985 by famed pro wrestler Satoru "Tiger Mask" Sayama and although the rules are slightly different from the UFC, it has created a number of major stars, including: Takanori Gomi, Rumina Sato, Hayato Sakurai, Anderson Silva, Enson Inoue and Erik Paulson. Shooto continues to host events all over the world in the US, Europe, and of course Japan. Though it was started by Sayama, there has never been one worked match in the promotion's history.

PANCRASE

Pancrase was started by another stiff-worked shoot wrestler named Masakatsu Funaki, but the majority of the matches were real and the fights were executed with open hand palm strikes—not fists. The early days of Pancrase was a who's who of MMA legends including Ken Shamrock, Bas Rutten, Frank Shamrock, Guy Mezger and Semmy Schilt. Formed months earlier than the UFC in 1993, Pancrase was a breakaway hit and was so popular that SEG actually purchased Pancrase shows and ran them on pay-per-view to coincide with their UFC events at the time. Eventually Pancrase moved to closed-fist fights with four-ounce gloves after Rings did the same, but the fights had less rules than the UFC leading to quite a few devastating knockouts. Pancrase is still around today, but after so many of its stars left, most of the cards are composed of up and coming Japanese talent.

KING OF THE CAGE (KOTC)

Started in 1998, some would consider KOTC the biggest "feeder show" in the world, as a huge number of today's top MMA stars have fought their way through the promotion, including current UFC light heavyweight champ Quinton "Rampage" Jackson and *The Ultimate Fighter's* Diego Sanchez. KOTC is one of a handful of organizations that has managed to constantly host successful events all over the world in the US, Canada, Australia and Singapore.

With the mainstream appeal of the UFC created by The Ultimate Fighter, the sport has grown in all directions, especially with new US promotions. Boxing promoter Gary Shaw and Showtime started **EliteXC** to promote their own events and partner with existing promotions. **The International Fight League** promotes all over the US with teams germane to specific regions. **Strikeforce** set the all-time attendance record for North America with its debut show in San Diego. Billionaire Calvin Ayre's **BodogFight** gang-shoots fights in exotic locations for its television shows. Dallas-based **Art of War** promoted a major pay-per-view event its third fight out and is one of the few publicly traded companies in the business. With more players entering the game and an ever-increasing talent pool, the fastest growing sport isn't stopping and no matter what happens in the ring, the fans never lose.

Super Natural

Interview by
RJ Clifford

Count him out, say he's too old and make excuses, but let's face it: there is only one Captain America in this sport. In his last heavyweight title defense, Couture imposed his will and took the imposing Gabriel Gonzaga into dark waters...bloody dark waters and handed him his second loss. He took some kicks and punches along the way, but "The Natural" stayed methodical with his approach and frustrated the Brazilian contender.

Just two days after his big win, MMA Worldwide sat down with Couture to

MMA WORLDWIDE: Okay, so the big question on everyone's mind… Gonzaga's broken nose?

RANDY COUTURE: I believe it happened on the takedown in the first round when I picked him up and took him down with the high single. We came down very, very hard with both our bodyweights. Our heads collided when he hit the mat, my head was close to his head and I heard his nose crunch in my ear. When we scrambled up to our feet at that point, I noticed all the blood so that's when I thought it happened. I mean we exchanged a lot of punches. I hit him with a straight jab and a left hook right off the bat that wobbled him a little bit. I suppose it could have happened somewhere else, but that's when I felt like it happened and the impact of that takedown was very, very big.

MW: Do you feel you took Gonzaga out of his game plan being that aggressive and that he wasn't prepared for it?

RC: Well I hope that's what I did. I don't expect that his game plan was to be pressed against the fence, hit and taken down the way he was taken down. We traded some, which I'm sure is more in line with his game plan. I'm sure he thought I would try to take him down earlier and he would be more effective or have enough gas to be more effective once it hit the ground. I felt comfortable with the game plan of pushing the pace, using the clinch, using the dirty boxing—all the things I trained to do worked very well. My hand skills and head movement were good and made it hard for him to hit. He's very explosive. His high kick was very surprising with how quickly he could throw that.

MW: He landed a couple punches and kicks, one big kick in particular. Did any of them rock you?

RC: He actually didn't hit me with his shin; he hit me with his foot. He just kind of slapped me. It probably looked a lot worse than it was. There was one punch that I saw stars off of, but recovered pretty dang quickly and didn't feel like I was in danger. The times he did hit me, I responded right away by closing the distance and getting back to where I wanted to be which was in his face.

MW: Did one of those kicks break your arm?

RC: The last kick before the fight ended in the third round, I checked it off my arm and broke the smaller bone in my arm, the ulna. I had a suspicion something was wrong with it when it happened. We ended up in the clinch right

Randy with his wife Kim.

Randy and his team working his booth.

9

after that and then I took him down and ended the fight. They examined me after and it felt OK; there was a bruise and a bump there and I thought it was just a real good bruise where he hit me. By later that evening and the next morning, it was very, very swollen. I couldn't move my hand so I figured the bone was probably broken. I got an X-ray and confirmed what I suspected.

MW: How long will that keep you out of commission?

RC: I won't be able to train a whole lot for six weeks. I'll be wearing a splint for the next six weeks. The small bone prognosis is very good. They heal very strong and the bone is not displaced so no surgeries or anything. I'm not even in a cast, just a splint. It's very sore and very swollen now, but it will start sticking together and re-healing in just over a week. In two weeks, it's pretty bonded and as long as I don't bang it or knock it around, it'll be alright.

MW: Where would you rank your striking at this point?

RC: I don't know, rate it with who, rate it with what? I certainly know I have spent a lot of time there and I have some great trainers in that area and it has gotten a lot better. It's not my expertise so it's probably not my place to be rating it. I think it is certainly effective and allows me to do what I need to do to win fights. It's an area I have a lot of fun learning and I will continue to train that area and fashion that part of my game. It allows me to take advantage of my wrestling and mat skills.

MW: Do you think at some point you will stop being labeled the underdog?

RC: I don't think that's going to happen and that's OK with me; it doesn't bother me any. It puts me in a place first of all where I don't have a lot of pressure to go out and perform or do anything. I can just go out and do what I do which is what I like anyway. It seems I respond really well when people say, "Oh, he's not going to do that" or "He can't beat him." That just makes me train that much harder and get the job done.

MW: Is Fedor who you want next and do you have a list of guys you want to fight?

RC: I don't have a list at all. Certainly Fedor being the Pride heavyweight champion and what most people consider as the number one fighter in the world. Those are the guys you want to fight and if that happens, great, if it doesn't, that's OK too. I don't have a list. I just want interesting fights. I love to compete and he would be the pinnacle of competition right there.

MW: What about Antonio "Minotauro" Nogueira?

RC: I have always had a lot of respect for Minotauro's ability. I think he's a great fighter. I've cornered Dan Henderson with both his fights against Minotauro. I've watched him fight Heath Herring and I've seen a lot of his fights over the years. He's a great fighter and a great submission guy. Whatever the company decides should happen and should be the next fight in the heavyweight division, I'll be ready.

MW: Light heavyweight?

RC: I have no idea. If they made me an offer to go down and it was an intriguing match-up, then that could happen. I can make 205. We'll just have to see where the offers come from and what they want to do with me. I'm having a great time.

MW: Are you looking to build a big, competitive team with Xtreme Couture like AKA or the old Team Quest, or are you just

Part of the team of Extreme Couture.

Randy and Chuck Zito hanging out at Extreme Couture.

trying to surround yourself with good guys to train with?

RC: First and foremost, you need good guys and good training. That's all I really care about and I think we are attracting those kinds of people. We're looking for individuals with that kind of like-mindedness, work ethic and character. I don't measure myself to AKA or Team Quest or anyone else. We are doing what we do and trying to do it right, be positive and have fun. Those guys are my family.

MW: What are your thoughts on Dan Henderson and Rampage Jackson?

RC: Good fight, very tough fight. One of those fights you have trouble picking since you can make a case for either guy to go out and win. The more of a wrestling match that Dan makes it, the better for him; his wrestling pedigree is second to none. I think the more of a boxing match or striking match that Rampage can make it; the better it will be for him. The only problem is they both have a tendency to operate in the other area. Rampage likes to try and slam people while Danny likes to go out and try to punch people in the head and go nose to nose. It will be interesting to see who fashions a successful game plan and who goes out and implements it in the fight. It's going to be a wild fight!

MW: Rampage spent some time training with you in Las Vegas correct?

RC: No, he came in for a weekend. He has come in the gym on several occasions, but he does all his training up in Big Bear. He was in doing a photo shoot with Cheick Kongo and Michael Bisping for the card and he trained at the gym for like three days, but that was the extent of his exposure at Xtreme Couture. I think Rampage's camp put out some misinformation that I was training him for Dan and that's not really accurate.

MW: How do you balance a family, gym, business ventures and a career?

RC: I have a very supportive wife and a great staff at Xtreme Couture that help juggle all the balls. They help me take care of all that stuff and allow me to focus on training when I need to train and being prepared for a fight and keep everything else up in the air and running. It's a good situation and it's nice to have that support.

MW: Talk about your role in *Red Belt.*

RC: *Red Belt* was a blast first of all. I got to play a commentator which wasn't a very big stretch for me considering the last year that's all I've been doing. I had a great experience working with David Mamet, a very well known writer and director. He does things a little bit differently than the other film experiences I've had. He changes things on the fly, has a very keen sense for actors and working with actors. He's taught me some things and brought up things, skills that I didn't have before that experience.

MW: What do you have on your plate for the next couple of months?

RC: Well I'm at the MAGIC show right now for the clothing line Xtreme Couture with Affliction and it's off the chain. The clothing line is just blowing up and has gone way faster than we predicted. We are doing our best to keep up with demand. It is very, very exciting and the line looks fantastic. I'm shooting another episode of *The Unit* with David Mamet. The TV series airs in about a week and a half. I will be in South Africa for the month of October because I have a lead role in the prequel of *The Scorpion King* where I'll be playing the bad guy.

MW: Will your broken arm influence your role in that movie?

RC: It's five weeks away so I should be OK.

MW: Anything you want to say to your fans?

RC: Just that I really appreciate the support. Make sure everybody checks out the new association with www.mmaworldwide.com and all the benefits the association will bring in. The Fight Lab, a new company out of Canada that is booking fighters, will have some big deals on the horizon with that. Couture Nutrition and Xtreme Couture gyms and clothing lines are doing very well and that is due to the fans and their support.

For more information on Randy Couture, check out www.thenatural.tv and www.mmaworldwide.com

Randy "The Ninja" Couture

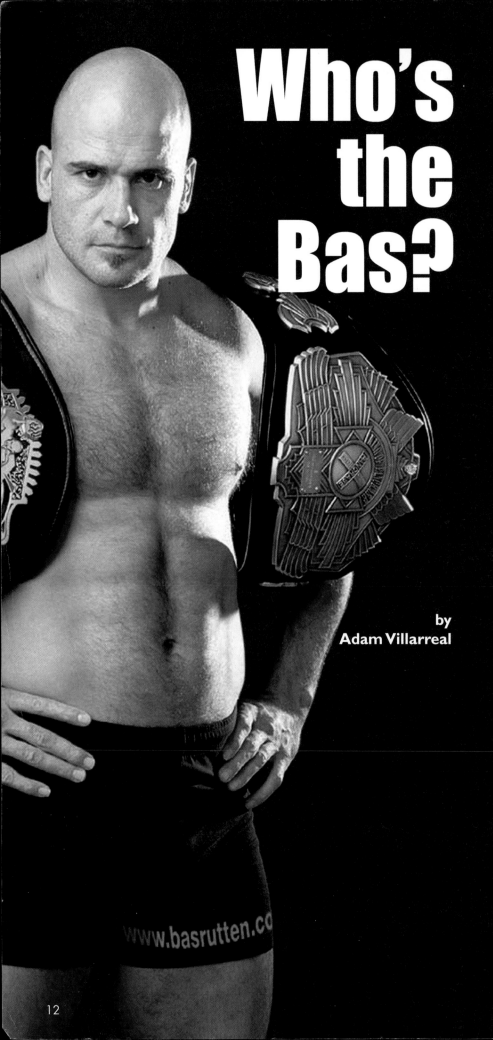

Who's the Bas?

by
Adam Villarreal

Bas Rutten has solidified himself as a mixed martial arts pioneer with his well-documented resume that boasts a UFC heavyweight championship, in addition to being a three-time undefeated King of Pancrase champion. Being the consummate class act, he was kind enough to sit down and share some thoughts, memories and predictions about his family and fight career.

If you're a Rutten fan, you're more than likely aware of his childhood in the Netherlands. He even likes sharing those details about his upbringing. "Well as you can read on my website, I have a real loving family; the opposite of me, so I am the black sheep. As most people know, I had a very bad skin disease and very bad asthma growing up. It was so bad I'd have to spend a week in bed sometimes. With a skin disease, I'd have to wear gloves and I wouldn't look really good, so of course I didn't have a lot of friends."

"As I grew up, I spent a lot of time by myself and my biggest thing to do was going into the forest and climbing trees. When I was bullied, I'd climb into trees where no one could follow me. I had this whole path through the entire woods and I would climb into one tree and I could go to the other side of the woods without touching the ground.

From kickboxer to performer to MMA fighter, Rutten has ran the gauntlet of physical challenges. Aside from facing an army of opponents in the ring, Bas entered into the dangerous and painstaking world of fatherhood. "I have a 18-year-old daughter in Holland and she's with my ex-wife, and I have two girls here with my wife now. I've been with her for 16 years already, which is something unbelievable; living with Bas Rutten for 16 years! She's a keeper and the kids are really cool. My 10-year-old wants to be a dancer and singer, and my youngest one is a little boss.

Rutten expressed his outlook on fatherhood and marriage in a charming way, though he realizes his two youngest daughters aren't ready to start dating. But I shoot from the hip. We'll see what happens and I'll take it from there."

For now Bas is happy with the love and adoration he gets from the boys too young o knock on his door with flowers for his daughters, who seem just as happy with having 'El Guapo' for a dad. "You know, they're proud of it and they enjoy it. If I go to their school, the boys all know me so they're attacking me and it's fun. Here (America), they think it's great and the kids love it. That's why I love it here. I think the people here are way friendlier.

'Don't get me wrong, Holland is very nice too, but it's a small country like everything in Europe. They say stuff like, 'Oh, George Bush is a cowboy and he's like that because he's from Texas,' and I tell them, He was born in Connecticut and he's not a cowboy, so what's your second point?' They won't say anything. I've never had a problem here and I think you have more chances of success here with what you're doing. Over there I'd make a $1,000 for doing the same job over here that would pay $5,000."

Like any father and husband balancing a job that takes him around the world, he keeps his family close to his heart. "Family means everything. I mean everything goes around that and health; the health of my family. There's nothing you can do if your kids or wife get sick. You have control over everything else."

As we all know, Bas is a character and a personality like no other. I had a reporter here from Japan tell me that you could read a man by his musical taste and asked if he could look through my CD collection. About ten minutes later, he stopped and said I was a psychopath! I got everything.

With movies, there's a lot. Of course I like Pacino and Mickey Rourke. I saw *Sin City* and I thought it was a real good movie. *True Romance* is big on my list, and so is *Scarface*, which is on every fighter's list. I think those movies are fun, but I like epics too like *The Last Samurai*."

With his life outside the ring flourishing like never before, Bas is preparing for the inevitable day when the fighting and coaching stop for good. "You know, lately I've been thinking about it and I like fishing. That's something I wanted to do when I was 20 years old. So when I retire, maybe I'll have a boat and do it as a business. I like to talk to people and I like to have fun, and when people go fishing, they have a lot of fun because it's drinking and eating what you caught. I think that's a good combination."

"But when it is all over, I just hope people regard me as one of the first guys because we started before the UFC in Japan (Pancrase started nearly two months before the first UFC.) and we were the pioneers for everybody else. There's a legacy there! As long as they have some good stories about me, I'll be happy. I will still enjoy the good response I get from people and it's been great!"

Wherever Bas ends up, his contribution to MMA will never be forgotten. We hope to see more commentating and maybe even one last fight from 'El Guapo', but no matter what happens, he's still the Bas!

Dan Henderson: Two Down, One to Go

Interview by RJ Clifford and Bobby Pittman
Written by RJ Clifford

On December 9, 2000 in PrideFC, **Wanderlei Silva** ended American **Dan Henderson**'s nine-fight win streak, handing him his first professional MMA loss. Over six years later, they met again in the same show, but this time in the United States. Henderson avenged his first loss with a third round knockout, becoming the first fighter to hold belts in two weight divisions in a major organization simultaneously. With the demise of Pride, dan's next big challenge will be against UFC Light Heavyweight Champ Quinton "Rampage" Jackson for the belt on September 8, 2007 at UFC 75 in London.

Born in Downey, California, Henderson's childhood was, in his own words, "Fairly normal. I played baseball up to high school and wrestled. I grew up with horses and lots of animals, basically every animal you can think of." His wrestling career at Victor Valley High School included a second and fifth place finish in his junior and senior years respectively. He was also a high school national champion in freestyle and Greco-Roman, the two international styles of wrestling.

After a short stint in the collegiate ranks, Henderson made the move literally and figuratively to the international level. "At the end of 1991, I took a four month trip to Russia and that's pretty much the trip that put me over the top." The skills he developed overseas helped him qualify to

"I don't think any sport is as exciting as MMA."

represent the United States in the 1992 Olympics in Barcelona. Henderson not only came out of nowhere in the American wrestling scene and won the qualifying tournament, he did it at the tender age of 21. "I wasn't cocky, but I wasn't one of those guys (that thought) just because this guy is a returning world champ or Olympic champ that I'm supposed to lose. That follows through with my mentality that I get up for bigger challenges," he explains, a character asset that would serve him well in his MMA career.

Henderson fell short of medaling in '92, but after a shoulder surgery and qualifying for two more world teams, he was back in the Olympics again in 1996. After

going 1–2 in '96 and falling short of a medal again, Henderson started fighting MMA to pay the way for his wrestling career. "In '97, I started fighting MMA. One event down in Brazil and I won that no problems, then I fought in the UFC in '98, which was about three weeks before the world team trials. I ended up breaking my jaw (in the UFC) so I couldn't compete in the world team trials."

Even though Henderson failed to make the world team in 1999 and 2000, he did compete in Japan's tough Rings tournament. "I focused a lot more on my MMA after the Olympic trials in 2000. They brought me in as an alternate and

Henderson and Couture had been training together for five years prior to entering the MMA realm, creating the emergence of what would become Team Quest. Matt Lindland later moved back to Oregon from Nebraska and started training and fighting. "We had all expressed interest in fighting. There is zero money in wrestling. So we saw that as a way to make a little bit of money to keep wrestling basically. When I won that King of Kings tournament, I went from a $30,000 a year guy to the tournament win paying me $230,000. The final fight was worth $200,000 alone." As a fulltime fighter, Henderson has to admit MMA is more exciting than wrestling. "I

workout partner. After that I went to Japan to corner Randy (Couture) in his Rings tournament, came back to Australia, then back home, then to a wrestling tournament in France for a week. I was kind of in party mode and got sick after that. I had about 10 days of training before I fought my first Pride fight against **Wanderlei Silva.** I was really out of shape against Wanderlei and it showed. I made sure it didn't happen this time." Dan Henderson was no longer an international wrestler; he was a professional mixed martial artist.

don't think any sport is as exciting as MMA."

With two Pride championship belts, one has to wonder what is next for "Dangerous" Dan. First he will sit back and see what transpires with the upcoming Matt Lindland vs. Fedor Emelianenko bout in bodogFIGHT. "Matt's fight with Fedor is going to be an interesting match. I think everybody thinks that Matt has zero chance in that fight. I hope everyone thinks that, including Fedor. Matt surprises a lot of people with what he can do. Matt and I are similar in the mental aspect that we come up for bigger fights and this will be his toughest opponent yet. He is capable of finishing Fedor."

For those who follow the sport closely enough, you will start to notice a pattern with these crazy Oregon wrestlers. Randy Couture just went up a weight class to fight UFC champion Tim Sylvia, Matt Lindland is fresh off his fight with the powerful light heavyweight fighter Quinton "Rampage" Jackson and now plans on fighting up one *more* weight class for Fedor. Now Henderson wants to follow in Lindland's footsteps and challenge Fedor. One has to wonder what these guys are thinking. "Pride mentioned it would be a pretty good promotion if I challenge for a third belt. They do it in boxing all the time."

In between challenges against heavier opponents, the laidback Dan Henderson spends his time the way most people would if they owned a five acre plot of land in the middle of Temecula's wine country. "When I'm not training for a fight, I like to ride my horses, spend time with my kids and attend their sporting events, and hanging out with my friends." The kids he is speaking of are his six-year-old son Reese and his eight-year-old daughter Sierra.

Dan met Alison, the mother of his children, through a friend in high school. "We hung out all the time and she was her girlfriend. We started dating and started having kids." When asked if being a fighter helped seal the deal with his wife, he says casually, "No, at that point the biggest thing in my life was the fact that I was a two-time Olympian. I don't know if that helped (laughs), but I got her."

As the Pride welterweight Grand Prix champion, Pride welterweight champion and new Pride middleweight champion, the world is Henderson's oyster. With the likes of champions like Chuck Liddell still reigning well into their thirties, 36-year-old Henderson still has a lot of tread on his tires. When asked what he wants to be remembered for, he answers simply, "I want to be remembered for more than I've accomplished now. In other words, I'm not done yet."

For more information on Dan Henderson, log on to www.danhenderson.com.

17

QUINTON

Mr. Jackson
If You're Nasty

by Adam Villarreal

Quinton "Rampage" Jackson was one of the last men to defeat Chuck "The Iceman" Liddell. Since his UFC debut this past February, American fans are finding out more about the Memphis native who became a superstar in PRIDE. With his new contract and highly anticipated rematch against the Iceman on the horizon, we were lucky enough to sit down with the 28-year-old Rampage, a man never short on words.

MMA WORLDWIDE: How was life growing up?

QUINTON JACKSON: It was cool as hell you know, being that I was the black sheep of my family and a loner. My family couldn't stand my guts. I love them to death, but I have been living in California for six years and haven't been back to visit since then.

MW: Did you play any sports?

QJ: I wrestled for one and a half years in high school and that's the reason my wrestling sucks so bad. I played football for one year and I was a natural. I was the smallest nose guard in the league, but I got the job done so my coach made me team captain after like two weeks.

MW: What did you want to be when you were a child?

QJ: I wanted to be a pro wrestler or a stunt man. My favorite wrestler was the Ultimate Warrior. I would dress up as the Ultimate Warrior for every Halloween. I didn't know he was white, so it was pretty embarrassing when I found out I was trying to be like a white guy.

During his decision win over Matt Lindland.

ass kicked for a couple hours.

MW: What do you do on the weekends in your off time?

QJ: I like to sit at home and just rest, cause I am so beat up from training. I like to play videogames with my kids, but usually they just end up watching me play cause I am selfish.

MW: What kind of music do you

When he's not punching people he's playing video games.

MW: How many kids do you have?

QJ: I have four. They are all cute in their own ways. Two of them have bad breathe, but that's cause they take after their mom's side of the family.

MW: How hard is it to transition from being a fighter to a father?

QJ: It's just as difficult as the transition from being a lawyer to a fighter. It's my main job. I wake up every morning and take care of my kids and get them to school, and then I go and train and get my

listen to?

QJ: I listen to rap and hip-hop, gospel and Reggae.

MW: What's it like being a celebrity?

QJ: Sometimes I don't like it because I'm a private person and a regular guy. It can be annoying at times when you go out and people say dumb things.

MW: If you could live anywhere in the world, where would it be?

QJ: I would like to live in either Japan or Vancouver, Canada. In Vancouver, Hot Asian chicks dig black men like myself. In Orange County, I can't even get a girl to look at me. In LA, sometimes I can get girls to look at me, but never twice. I am a good looking guy I think; well at least that's what my mama told me.

MW: Where are you training out of right now?

QJ: I am training out of Huntington Beach Ultimate and BodyShop Fitness in Lakewood. They are the best two gyms in Southern California. Tiki runs HB Ultimate and Antonio McKee runs BodyShop.

MW: How's life in Cali?

QJ: I like it and I don't want to leave since my kids are in school. But one of my kid's teachers, I think she's new; she gets on my damn nerves!

MW: What's it like when you're home?

QJ: I noticed a little more attention now that I'm in the UFC rather than PRIDE. I do think the UFC's making a big mistake by having me fight Chuck Liddell next because people still really don't know who the hell I am. But who am I? I'm just some fighter right?

MATT HUGHES

A Country Boy Can Survive

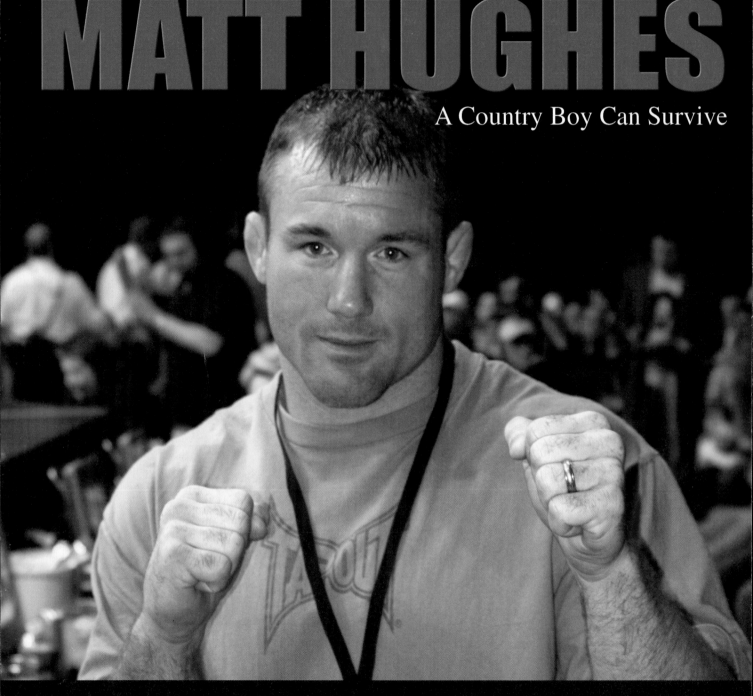

The most dominating welterweight in the history of the UFC, Matt Hughes has proven over and over again why many consider him one of the greatest fighters of all time. Having fought in over a dozen title fights, Matt has defeated the likes of Carlos Newton, Sean Sherk, BJ Penn, Georges St. Pierre and even MMA legend Royce Gracie. His popularity as a champion coupled with his popularity from coaching in UFC's reality show **The Ultimate Fighter** have made this Illinois native one of the most sought after farm boys in the fight game. Having overcome multiple obstacles in his career, Matt is constantly reminding us why the championship belt never looked at home unless it was around his waist.

If there is one fighter who represents what a UFC champion should be, it is Matt Hughes. A no-nonsense, blue-collar warrior, Hughes climbs into the Octagon with only one thought on his mind – to bring it on! Moving relentlessly forward, exerting constant pressure, and always putting his opponent in difficult positions, Hughes has a knack for dictating the pace of a match and making his opponent fight the way he wants them to. This in-your-face, take-no-prisoners mentality has made Hughes one of the UFC's most popular champions and brought worldwide acclaim to this native son of Hillsboro, Illinois. But Hughes hasn't let success go to his head. Still as accessible and down-to-earth as you'd expect someone from America's heartland to be, Matt Hughes seems destined to carry the UFC championship torch for years to come.

Q: What's your athletic background?

A: I played high school football, was a two-time state high school wrestling champion, two-time junior college All-American at Lincoln Junior College, and two-time Division 1 All-American at Eastern Illinois. After I finished college I started coaching at Eastern Illinois but I still wanted to compete. In 1997 some friends of mine told me about a small mixed martial arts show in Chicago at Madonna High with a one-hundred dollar prize. So I entered and fought Craig "The Terminator" Quick. I won pretty fast by taking him down, taking him to the fence and then just pounding him. After that first fight I thought there was no way that anyone in my weight class could keep me from taking them down. After five fights I hooked up with Monte Cox who became my manager. After 10 or so more fights I made it into the UFC in Lake Charles, Louisiana. I've just kept going since.

Q: How does wrestling and MMA training differ?

A: Technically speaking, my wrestling training just involved that sport, so it was pretty straightforward. But for ultimate fighting you have to train for knees, punches, elbows and everything else. In wrestling I was a natural, but learning stand-up fighting for MMA was difficult. A lot of wrestlers have a tough time going to their backs, but that didn't bother me at all. For a long time, I also had a tough time getting submissions. I was good on the practice mat but not in the cage. I've gotten a lot better, though, and now I actually look for submissions.

Q: What kind of physical training do you do?

A: I lift weights for about an hour a day, jog a half-hour a day in the morning, then also do hill sprints. For weight training I'll do reps of 12, 10, and 6 – so at the end I'll do six heavy reps for power and then one more light set for endurance. I don't really do a lot of bench press but do like working my back and shoulders. You don't use the chest a lot in wrestling and fighting. Arms also are not that important. More than anything else you do a lot of pulling. If you spend too much time trying to develop pure strength it will take away from your technical positions and your endurance, which are much more important.

Matt all decked out in our gear.

Q: Who has had the biggest influence on your fighting style?

A: Pat Miletich and Jeremy Horn. Pat's game is 90 percent stand-up but he is also great on the ground. Jeremy is a master on the ground and I've learned most of my submissions from him. A big part of my success is my training with Team Miletich – there are just so many tough guys there. Honestly, a lot of my gym training has been harder than my fights in the cage. Pat, Robbie Lawler, Jeremy and I go at it really hard in training. A fight is won in the gym.

Q: Do you think wrestling is the best background for MMA?

A: I think so. A wrestler can pick where the fight will end up – the ground or the feet. A striker is locked-in to keeping the fight standing. Wrestlers have given me the toughest times in fights. My match against Sean Sherk, a really good wrestler, was probably my toughest. Stand-up fighters can get taken out of their element easier. Against strikers, I try not to shoot-in blindly, keep my hands up, and then force them into the fence.

If I can get my hands on any striker I know I can take them down. Against submission or jiu-jitsu fighters I either keep the fight on the feet and defend their takedowns, or I can go to the ground, get inside their guard, and then pound them. That was how I fought Renato Verissimo, who is a great submission fighter. I don't think the guard is that great of a position in the cage. Sometimes you have to use it, of course, but as an offensive strategy people have caught onto it and it isn't that effective anymore.

Q: How do you mentally focus before a fight?

A: I've competed so much in my life that I have tunnel vision and only think about my opponent. So I don't really get rattled or emotional. I stay very focused and calm and keep my head on my shoulders.

Q: Are you satisfied with your current fighting style?

A: If you want to be a successful fighter you can never feel that way. I'm always learning and growing. Pat is still learning. Jeremy is still learning. I learn something new every day. The sport has so many facets that you have to be mentally open. The Matt Hughes of today is much better than the Matt Hughes of five years ago, and the Matt Hughes of five years from now will be much better than the Matt Hughes of today.

Q: Will the sport grow?

A: The UFC is the single greatest fighting event in the world and it will continue to increase. It has boxing, wrestling, jiu-jitsu, kickboxing and more all rolled into one. There's already talk that it will be on the Fox Network and Spike TV live. Eventually, you'll see MMA grow much bigger than boxing. For me, MMA started out purely as a hobby and I did it for fun. Now, seven years later, I have become a champion and it's a way of life and my primary source of income. That shows how far the sport has come in only a few years.

Q: What is a champion?

A: My definition of a champion is that if your back is up against the wall – even if you've lost a match or two and everyone thinks you're done – a true champion will find a way to come back and somehow find a way to win.

DEEP FREEZE

by John Stewart
Interview by Bobby Pittman

Nine years ago, Chuck Liddell was on shaky ground with a volatile sport. He made a few thousand bucks fighting in SEG's last days of owning the UFC and even banged it out bare-knuckle style in a lone match in Brazil. With his ice-cold eyes and mohawk, Liddell was surprisingly media shy and quiet, preferring to do all his business in the cage.

Today Liddell is the first mainstream sports star in mixed martial arts. He has proven himself time and time again, knocking out nearly every opponent he's faced. His fan base grows weekly due to all the appearances and seminars that take up most of his time. Of course there are the thousands of fans trying to pat him on the back as he walks down the ramp and the unlucky millions of fans who can only watch him on TV. Liddell was also the first MMA star to sign a million dollar endorsement contract, and with fight purses and bonuses, he's making the money that most thought would never happen in this "fringe" sport. And though he's been spotted with his share of celebrity girlfriends, Liddell has managed to stay grounded. He's also more talkative.

On January 8, 2007, just over a week after defeating Tito Ortiz a second time, *MMA Worldwide* tracked down the Iceman at the Standard Hotel in Los Angeles. We wanted to learn more about his personal life, digging up some of his past in the process. With so many fighters saying all they do is sleep and train, we decided to have Liddell break down a day for us. "Well, I was at home for 12 hours. I flew to Florida, now I'm in LA today and I fly to New York tomorrow. You know I probably would have bitched and moaned about it, if it wasn't for the fact I got to have breakfast with my daughter Trista this morning. I woke up and she asked me, 'Daddy, you want me to make you pancakes?' I was like all right, yeah (smiles). We got in at 2:30 in the morning and probably didn't get to bed until 3:00. But I drove over to her house at 6:30 AM and had breakfast with her before she went off to school."

Between workouts and being the face of the UFC, Liddell has always been there for his kids, but sometimes he has to put it in high gear. When faced with the possibility of missing his son Cade's birthday over attending a seminar, the Iceman decided to have his cake (literally) and eat it too. "I flew into Denver, got a car, got to his house at 1:00 in the afternoon. Then he showed up at about 4:00 (he was at another birthday party). I left his house at 4:00 AM and drove to the airport to fly back out. But I'll tell you man, the look on his face when he saw me was priceless. His mom decided to surprise him and I brought his sister with me, my daughter. I wasn't even in Denver for 24 hours, but I got to spend his whole birthday with him and with the look on his face, I would have done it 100 times."

With MMA being a young sport with young fans, it's no surprise that Liddell has become a role model for kids, sometimes in the strangest of ways. Just before the rematch with Ortiz, Liddell flew to Ohio to visit a young boy who had just contracted leukaemia. Upon showing up with his daughter, Liddell learned that the boy's parents had saved up money to take him out to dinner with their son as a show of gratitude. "I was like, 'You guys are kidding me right? Let me get this. I got this.' We went to Applebees and I was eating my vegetables, since I eat those first, then I go to my rice and then my chicken. I had a couple of things that came up for the UFC, but I was like, 'You know, this kid's got leukaemia. I can't wait till after the fight. If I never got to see the kid after promising him I was coming, I'd never forgive myself.' So I took off after training one day and went up there." Liddell still keeps in contact with the family today. "The weirdest thing for me was, they said that's how they get him to eat his vegetables, because I did. 'The

Iceman does. The Iceman eats his vegetables. You gotta eat yours.' It was just weird seeing some parent use me as an influence on their kids."

Liddell remembers when he was that age and hardly the fighter he is today. "I was one of two white kids in my class. I was getting beat up everyday and I wouldn't fight back. So the teacher asked me, 'Hey, why don't you defend yourself?' I guess I told him that my mom told me I couldn't fight. So he went to my mom and told her, 'Hey, you've got to let this kid defend himself. He's getting beat up everyday.' It's amazing how things change.

Liddell started wrestling during his sophomore year in high school and eventually became freestyle state champion. He served on the starting line-up for Cal Poly University for four years in a row and got an accounting degree as well. In 1992, Liddell felt the competition itch and met John Hackelman, who trained him in kempo karate. Hackelman, a former pro boxer and veteran kickboxer, has been his trainer ever since.

During a local kickboxing smoker, Liddell earned the name "Iceman" and it's stuck with him, much like his mohawk. That all started when Liddell and some friends from college went to a Slayer concert. Everyone was going to shave their heads, something Liddell would never have been able to do in high school. "With my grandpa, it was high and tight. But in college, there was no

fuckin' way I'm going back to the high and tight. I had always wanted a mohawk and that's what I ended up doing. I was 21 years old, and though I grew it out a couple of times, it's been that long."

Putting his accounting career on hold, Liddell started working out with an old college wrestling friend, Scott Adams, who eventually started World Extreme Cagefighting. Adams and Liddell took submission wrestling classes together, and after his first UFC fight, Liddell began taking $100 privates as a gift from BJJ black belt and UFC alumni John Lewis. Both men have graced Liddell's corner many times over. He is one of the few fighters out there who has kept a consistent training camp and the results are obvious.

With the drama and grudge with Tito Ortiz over, Liddell now sets his sights on Quinton "Rampage" Jackson, who became a UFC fighter when Zuffa purchased his contract from the now defunct World Fighting Alliance. "Quinton's back. That's the last loss on my record back in 2003. It's my last loss to avenge. (Liddell returned to avenge early losses to Jeremy Horn and Randy Couture, the only other men to hold wins over him.) And hopefully some new guys. There's some talent out there.

There's always new guys coming up and you've got to keep testing yourself."

Liddell has dominated the light heavyweight division, and with Mirko "Cro-Cop" now entering the UFC, there is talk of Liddell fighting in the heavies someday. "With either Cro-Cop or a guy like Fedor, I've really got nothing to lose.

Fedor would be a huge fight if that ever happens and it would be worth it for the fans. And it would be worth it for me because it's testing myself. I'm not afraid of anybody and I think I actually match up pretty well with Fedor. Don't get me wrong, I think he's a bad man. He is a bad man. He's one of the best in the world, if not THE best."

When he's not gunning for someone in the Octagon, Liddell likes to kick back with his favorite drink, Grey Goose and Red Bull. Though he's not out on the town as much anymore, one can still find Liddell frequenting a bar in San Luis

Obispo, just as easy as he can be found in Las Vegas or Los Angeles. Liddell doesn't have a particular type of food he enjoys most, but when the subject turned to movies, one stuck out. "The thing I always make people watch is the first five minutes of *Way of the Gun*. It's fuckin' hysterical. Have you seen it? Just watch the first five minutes." Musically speaking, Slayer is still in the mix, but Liddell also enjoys Lars and the Bastards, Pantera and Hank Williams Jr. "I've asked twice to come out to Pantera's *Walk*, but [Zuffa] won't let me."

"You come into this world with your word and your honor and you are the only one who can take it away from yourself before you go."

Mere mortals listen to music, watch movies and go clubbing, but superstar fighters like Chuck Liddell have their toys and that means fast cars. His favorite would have to be a $200,000 Ferrari F430 Spider. "That fuckin' thing is retarded. Retarded fast! If I don't kill myself in that thing—SHIT!" That's quite a difference from Liddell's first ride, a Ford Fairmont Station Wagon, given to him by his grandpa. The F430 Spider is just one of Liddell's toys, but he's out of the motorcycle game. "I had an XT 600 Enduro, but they talked me out of motorcycles after Frank Mir's accident. Thing is, he had only been riding for six months. That's one of the things about driving my Ferrari now. I drive it like I used to ride a motorcycle. I'm very defensive. I'm like, 'Ok, that car could come right now and make a mistake.'" To show just how far Liddell has come, his first big paycheck from a fight ($60,000 for two matches in one month) netted him an Expedition with 20-inch rims, and he thought that was something.

Recently signing a lucrative deal with Warner Bros. to push their mega-epic *300*, Liddell sits at the forefront of a sport destined to take over boxing as the number-one fighting sport in the world. And he has no plans of really retiring.

"I'm going to stay in the fight game as long as I can. I'll help out, if it needs it by then. I don't know if it will. There are so many kids now, like five-year-olds who know my name. They come up to me like, 'Hey Chuck.' There are kids that age doing MMA. I can't wait to see how those guys fight. I think that progression is going to be wonderful. It's great for the sport."

Liddell is quick to mention that even he is still learning. The old school "style vs. style" doesn't hold muster anymore. "Hey, anything you want to show me, I'll try it. You want to show me a workout program, I'll try it. You have a submission you want to show me, I'll try to learn it because I want to be able to teach it to somebody. I might not use it, but one of my guys might."

Liddell has reached a mainstream level few can surmise, but has remained humble. When asked for words of advice for fans and fighters alike, he quickly answered, "Just follow your dreams man. You know, do what you wanna do. Have fun in life. You only get one of 'em."

"I was one of two white kids in my class. I was getting beat up everyday and I wouldn't fight back. So the teacher asked me, 'Hey, why don't you defend yourself?'

Gina Carano: Not Just Another Pretty Face

by Adam Villarreal

"What happens in Vegas, stays in Vegas!" But outside of the glitz and decadence live real people living real lives. Like any place on the map, there is a grind fueled by those trying to make it and succeed in their respective fields. Enter Gina Carano.

Born in the midst of a Texas tornado and bearing the pedigree of having a former Dallas Cowboy football player as a father (Glen Carano), Gina flourished in your standard childhood activities like dance and gymnastics. Upon her parents divorce, she made the journey with her mother and two sisters to Las Vegas where her star would soon be discovered in Muay Thai, and ultimately the MMA world.

"I've been a serious tomboy my whole life. While my sisters were getting dressed up like ballerinas, I was dressing like a little football player," she said of her natural progression into a male-dominated sport.

Her career still budding and youthful, it will possibly lead her into something different later in life, as she has expressed a deep and keen interest in the arts such as writing and music. I also love to write poems, but I call them songs. One day, sooner than later, I will be getting more involved in some way with music. I always wanted to play the drums, so when I was 15, my mom got me a drum set. I started taking lessons, but got too involved with school and sports.

In my house it will just be my babies and I living here, and we are a wonderful trio! Their names are Gotti and Layla, two pitbulls who are exactly like me; they need more discipline in their life, they rebel against abused power, they're easily taught when intentions are right, they're playful but perfectly capable of taking care of business if it calls for it, they love to be loved, they love to love...and they're extremely protective of the people they love."

Beginning June 2006, Gina began competing in MMA and has won all three of her matches thus far, including a TKO over previously undefeated Rosi Sexton.

Like any girl, Gina likes to have fun and be around people who mold her into the positive woman she's become. At age 25, she's already feeling the beckoning of motherhood and the trials of relationships. "I'm calming down from dating or I should say serious relationships. I've had two serious relationships in the last six years. I'm not going to lie; I do want kids and this has all been in the recent year. If you would have asked me this two years ago, I would have told you, 'Hell No!' Right now I'm getting my priorities straight, so maybe in five years or so."

Her schedule and recent victories don't afford her the time for motherhood, though they definitely give her a reason to celebrate and enjoy her success. I like to have fun, but going clubbing is only fun occasionally. It gets old pretty fast, but I do like to hang out and meet new people. I love to watch live music, and I am not one of those judgmental music people who know every popular artist. I just like what I like.

Like so many people, she finds it important to step away and get back to the things that make her happy. "My perfect summer would be to hit Lake Tahoe as much as possible and stay on the lake. San Diego is the place we go to hang out at the beach, and we love it there." She adds, "The perfect winter for me would be to make as many snowboarding trips as possible.

Her athleticism shines through in her professional and personal life, but she also has a strong heart that puts people first. She's moved by acts of goodness and by the best intentions of people and sometimes strangers. She generally defines success as being able to look back and be happy about what you've done and where you've been and being able to be proud of it all.

If you haven't figured it out yet, I am a dreamer and I live in my head. I have found that dreaming is one thing that is mine and no one elses. I think people try to destroy each other's dreams all the time and most people let it happen, but when you stop and think about it, those dreams are yours and who's to tell you they aren't? Fighting has inspired my dreams, and now I think exactly like I did when I was a little girl because I believe that the reason I am doing what I love to do now is because I believed in it so much when I was younger. So if I keep dreaming now, I will be saying the same thing when I am 40 and so on."

She definitely bears the genetics and knows how to start the next generation of MMA fighters coming out of Las Vegas; either that or live the simple life with a husband and a few kids and dogs running around.

Gina with Elaina

Baby Gina with Mom and older sis

Gina kickin' it

Gina and Dad

Starting her career with famed Thai coach Master Toddy in Las Vegas

27

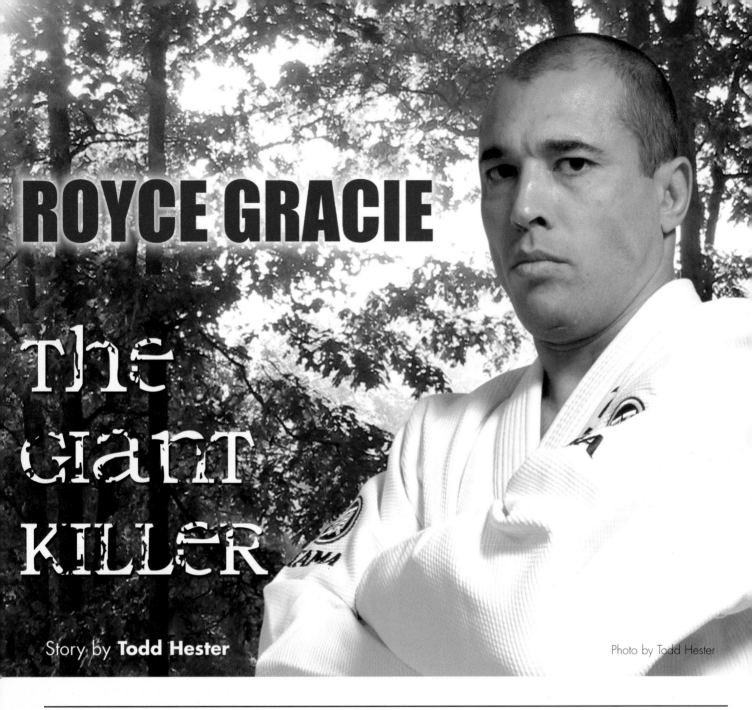

ROYCE GRACIE

The Giant Killer

Story by **Todd Hester**

Photo by Todd Hester

In an age where fighters refuse to face an opponent who misses making weight by a single pound, Royce Gracie is a throwback to an earlier time of honor and courage.

Fighting to prove the effectiveness of Gracie jiu-jitsu as his father originally envisioned, Royce Gracie has carried the family torch for over a decade and become the most famous and popular no-holds-barred fighter in the world. In 19 fights, with three draws and only one real loss, Royce has given up an average of 55 pounds to his opponents. The most experienced fighter in the world in matches against bigger foes, Royce took this art to a

new level when he fought 490-pound Sumo Grand Champion Akebono in Japan. Despite giving up over 300 pounds, Royce was able to take the fight to the ground and submit the 6'8" titan from the bottom in only two minutes and thirteen seconds. "To beat somebody smaller is not such a big thing," says Royce. "But to use your techniques and skill to beat someone larger – that is something special."

Q: What was the initial concept behind the development of Gracie jiu-jitsu?
A: The whole idea was for a smaller person to be able to survive an attack by a larger person. Not necessarily to beat him, but to not get hurt by him and to neutralize the attack. As a smaller person you have a chance to beat the bigger person – but the first goal is to stop the attack so the bigger person can't hurt you.

28

Q: When the UFC first started in 1993, was it a true reflection of this concept?

A: Yes, because there weren't any weight classes. It was as close as you could get to a real fight – no rules, no time limits, no gloves, no judges, no decisions, and no draws. Two men walk into the Octagon and one man walks out the winner. Everything goes and you just see what happens.

Q: Did it ever bother you to fight under those conditions – where everyone you fought was much larger than you?

A: It was not a problem at all. I loved it. It was such a challenge. To beat somebody smaller is not such a big thing. In nature, that is how it's supposed to be. The smaller and weaker are overcome by the bigger and stronger. But to reverse nature and use your techniques and your skill to do the opposite – to beat someone larger – that is something special. You're changing the course of nature.

Q: What happened when the UFC started to change the rules with time limits, judges and weight classes?

A: I think that it went away from its original purpose. The first reason that my brother Rorion started the UFC was what my father always had in mind – to show the jiu-jitsu techniques in action – how a smaller man can handle a larger opponent. That is why there were so many different styles originally in the UFC. There were grapplers, kickboxers, boxers, karate masters, judo players, kung-fu fighters, muay Thai fighters,

brawlers, you name it. Back then it was style against style. It wasn't the size that mattered but rather what you could do with what you knew. It was a true measure of which style was most effective in a real fight.

Q: How did the new rules effect the original UFC fans?

A: I don't think it really mattered. The fans kept following the sport. Back then they cheered for the style and now they cheer for the athlete. Now it is a measure of which man is better prepared.

Q: Which jiu-jitsu techniques work best against bigger opponents?

A: What I use is the basics. If you watch all my fights you will see the basics. I have the foundation and I have a good defense so I don't get hit. I don't need to get hit to show I'm tough; I prefer not to get hit. A lot of people only practice their offensive of how to hit someone or how to submit someone – but against a bigger opponent your defense should always come first. You have to survive the guy and neutralize him before you can take him down and submit him. If I'm on the bottom then I'm going to put him into my guard. I don't want to be on the bottom – if I can I will be on the top. That is my preference. A lot of people have said that I like to fight from the bottom, but that's not true. In the first three UFCs I always fought from the top. It was only in the final match of the fourth

UFC, against Dan Severn, that I fought from the bottom.

Q: What keeps you from getting intimidated when fighting a larger opponent?

A: It's knowing what I can do, knowing how far I can go, knowing my opponent, and knowing that I'm prepared and can walk up to him before the match and talk to him calmly and with confidence – like I did in Hawaii. I was there with Rodrigo for his fight and I saw Akebono sitting in the hotel lobby. I tapped him on the shoulder, stared him in the face, and said, "Yep, I think I'm definitely too big for you." Then I turned around and walked away, leaving him with a puzzled expression on his face (laughs).

Q: What was your toughest vale tudo fight?

A: I would have to say against Dan Severn in the UFC. He was a huge guy, 100 pounds heavier than me, and strong as an elephant. He had just been destroying everyone. People were afraid that I might get hurt or even killed. He got on top of me early and attacked me for 15 minutes straight. In the tape you can hear the announcers screaming, "Gracie is getting killed! Severn is destroying him! This fight needs to be stopped before Royce is seriously hurt!" But I kept using my basics; kept him in my guard; kept using my hips. Finally, when he got tired, I slid my hips out, climbed my legs up his back, and locked in the triangle choke. One second the announcers are screaming, "Royce is getting killed." Then the next second you hear, "What happened? The fight just ended! The referee stopped it! Severn tapped out! Royce wins! Royce wins!" That is Gracie jiu-jitsu in action.

Royce Gracie kicking to the leg of Akebono.

Antonio Rodrigo Nogueira

A Moment with Minotauro

by RJ Clifford

Arguably the greatest heavyweight fighter in the world not named Fedor, Minotauro has unleashed his Brazilian jiu-jitsu skills on fighters for years, twisting limbs and redirecting blood flow in his opponent's necks. As a member of the prestigious Brazilian Top Team, "Big Nog" is coming to the UFC. At UFC 69, "Minotauro" was reintroduced to the US to a throng of cheers from American fans. Excited about showcasing his skills in America, he will look to make his run for the UFC heavyweight belt.

Antonio Rodrigo Nogueira was born on June 2, 1976, in Vitoria da Conquista, Bahia, Brazil. A member of a large family including his twin brother Rogerio, his other brother Julio, and his sisters Jamile and Juliana, Antonio enjoyed a simple Brazilian childhood. Like many young Brazilians, his first trek into martial arts started with judo at age five and continued for three more years. At age 10, tragedy struck the young future champion when a truck ran him over. He had a broken leg and broken ribs which perforated his liver and threatened his life. "The truck came in

reverse gear and threw me on the ground, passing over my body slowly. My brother Rogerio tried to pull me up, but he couldn't. I only had time to move my head off the wheel and felt that weight squeezing my chest." He would spend four days in a coma and almost one year in the hospital, but the tough Brazilian proved his resiliency and bounced back after a doctor advised him to restart judo.

While living in Salvador studying at an electronic school, the 14-year-old started boxing with childhood hero and CNB world champion Arcemio Topo, planting the seeds of his future fighting career. In 1995, he further expanded his training by finding his true calling: Brazilian jiu-jitsu. Three weeks into training, he won a white belt tournament knowing only how to throw and a few ground positions. His jiu-jitsu credentials continued from there, winning the Brazilian Championship in 1996 (Blue Belt) and 1998 (Brown Belt). He earned his black belt by winning the Pan American Championships.

With his submission game in the books, the new black belt turned his sights to the MMA world. In 1999, he traveled to the United States and met World Extreme Fighting promoter Jamie Levine. After winning his first fight, the 6'3" fighter decided to stay in America and concentrate on MMA fulltime. After that, the rest is history. Reeling off six consecutive wins in WEF and Rings, one of Japan's oldest fight promotions, Nogueira finally faced his first loss (by decision) against current Pride welterweight and middleweight champion Dan Henderson at the 1999 Rings King of Kings tournament. Nogueira would take top honors the following year in the same tourney and avenged his loss to Henderson (by submission) two years later. Moving back to Brazil, Nogueira joined the legendary Brazilian Top Team, home to Mario Sperry, Paulo Filho, Ricardo Arona and his twin brother.

After going undefeated in Rings before the organization's demise, the Brazilian made his debut in Pride in 2001 by triangle-choking MMA vet Gary Goodridge. The heavyweight's ground skills and tough skull carried him through another long string of victories in the Japanese promotion including a heavyweight title and one of the most brutal come-from-behind wins over Bob Sapp. His success led him to become one of the most popular foreign fighters in the promotion, leaving Nogueira with a funny memory. "Two girls in Japan followed our bus for several kilometers back to our hotel. It was very far, but they got there just by running."

Now "Big Nog" has made the move back to the United States to fight in the UFC. "I began my fighting career here in America. I fought three times here. All of my family and friends are in Florida. (America) is a good place to be because the sport is

my jiu-jitsu style to all the American fans. It's good for my career right now." With the credentials he brings to the Octagon, a title shot should not be too far off in the future. "After the UFC in England, they will decide who I will face." When asked if he had anyone in particular, Nogueira simply mentions, "There are some top fighters in the UFC heavyweight division, but I can face any of them. I will show some jiu-jitsu skills and some submissions to the UFC fans." And that he can. With a record of 29-4-1, 18 of his wins have come by way of submission.

The transition from the Pride ring to the UFC cage is not as simple as many might think. There is an entirely different atmosphere fighting in America compared to Japan. The US has a different fan compared to the thousands of Japanese followers who have seen him compete live. Nogueira's fabled guard has a new enemy in the cut-opening elbow attack. Moving from the ring to the cage is the transition many experts say will present the heavyweight with the greatest challenge, but he thinks differently. "In the cage, the fight happens more. In a ring, sometimes you have to stop the fight when guys fall out of the ring. Sometimes when guys get in trouble, they will stick their head out of the ring, but you can't do that in the cage. I think I like the style. I will make my style a cage style."

As excited as American fight fans are for the move, Nogueira is even more excited.

come here to watch a UFC, a lot of American fans know the submission game and they have educated themselves and I think that is a big reason why." Nogueira also likes the beaches and shopping in the states, admitting with a smile.

In the meantime he will continue training and enjoying his time playing with his dogs, surfing and traveling with his daughter. When asked if he wanted her to follow in his footsteps, he perks up and says, "Yes, for sure. I am very proud of the sport I do and I would love to have my kid

have success in it too. I have one daughter and she loves to play jiu-jitsu (smiles). When she was two years old, she asked me for a gi and I said, 'No, you are too young, maybe four years old.' So she is doing capoeira."

After his fighting career, the black belt wants to continue in the sport he loves and help those around him. "I want to stay in fighting. I have a lot of good students and want to bring that good talent from Brazil." Any advice for up and comers? "You need a good team to be the best. Most fighters just worry about training, training, training, but you need a good manager."

Until that time, the 31-year-old will look to make the same mark in the UFC as he did in Pride. "I'm excited to be here and I hope to give you some exciting matches like I did in Japan." Not as excited as we are

Photo: Daynin Dashefsky

BJ "The Prodigy" Penn

By Bobby Pittman and Mike Wear

Photos by Bobby Pittman and Daynin Dashefsky

TO: How did you get into martial arts?

BJ: My friends and I always used to go to my house and box, and just hang out. One day this tae kwon do instructor (Tom Callos), who did a couple jiu-jitsu lessons with Ralph and Cesar Gracie, moved like six houses down from me. He was done teaching TKD, but wanted to have some people to work out with. We were about 16 to 17 years old at the time. He asked my dad if he could get me and a couple of my friends to come and roll around with him. I was like, "No, that sounds like a waste of time." I had seen the UFC, thought Royce was cool, but didn't really care to do it, you know? He kept bugging my dad, who finally said, "BJ, just go

down there so this guy leaves me alone." So it ended up that I went down there, and this guy choked me out, tapped me out, and from there, I just knew I liked it.

TO: When did you start competing?

BJ: Tom was doing something with his TKD instructor, so he took me up to Ralph Gracie's and I started training there. From there I just started competing after that. I was about 17 years old.

TO: How did you fare early on in competition, and when did you decide to make it a career?

BJ: I just started winning tournaments and doing the whole tournament scene. With jiu-jitsu, I never really took it serious. I just did it for fun and would never really get in shape for anything. Then I remember getting to the finals of the Black Belt World

Championships and I sat down and was like, "You know what, you'll never get this opportunity again to be right here in the finals making history, being the only non-Brazilian to ever win the BJJ World Championships. Go out there and no matter what, if your arm breaks or your leg breaks, just win this thing. Just go do it." That's when I really took it serious—winning that match.

TO: So what was the next step after that?

BJ: I was hanging out and met Dana White and Lorenzo Fertitta because they were taking privates from John Lewis. I worked out with them, and from there, they ended up buying the UFC. I knew them personally so I talked to Dana, and John Lewis talked to them to see if they could get me in the UFC. The rest is history.

TO: When did you realize you could be a world champion in MMA?

BJ: Well, my favorite fight of all time is probably my first fight in the UFC, just because that's like your first fight at the top level. I was thinking I wanted to see how I could do against someone who really is at the top. I beat Din, then Caol Uno. Jens Pulver was up next. I was thinking to myself, "You know what, I'm going to win this fight, get the belt and then I'm going to retire. It's done. My competitive career's done and that's it, it's over." So I ended up losing the fight against Pulver, and I guess that was good for me because I wouldn't have all this other stuff happening now. I was going to walk through that and then I'm gone, but MMA wasn't done with me.

TO: For the kid at home, you said he has to develop his own style, but if you had five minutes to tell him how to become a champ, what would you say?

BJ: I would tell him the first thing you do is go out and become a black belt in BJJ, then start adding takedowns to your game. Then get your wrestling to the highest level you can, go out and train as much as you can with the best wrestlers you can find anywhere in the world. After that, make your hands the icing on the cake. I'm sure a guy like Cro Cop will tell you something different.

TO: When do things start to calm down before the fight and the hard workouts end?

BJ: Ten days out. Maybe one or two workouts, but the time is cut short. I'll do three-minute rounds instead of five-minute rounds. Then I take the last six days off and peak myself getting ready for my fight.

TO: The win over Hughes was your biggest fight to date, but a lot of people counted you out.

BJ: I came into my own as a fighter and as a human being. When my last fight with Uno went to a draw, everybody said, "Oh you did well in that fight. You should have won." No. That wasn't the champion that BJ Penn wanted to be. Of all the hard work I've done in my whole life, you think I'd want to be the champion after a fight like that? No, I wouldn't want the belt after a fight like that. After the fight, I was like, "You know, I'm done already." I took a year off, which I definitely think people should do. I took a year off because I was taking fighting too professional, thinking it's all got to be done a certain way. I realized you're a human being first and a fighter second. I wasn't doing all those normal things that people do. I was cutting all those things off for fighting. On that year off I started living my life again normally, and then I had the (Takanori) Gomi fight. I hadn't fought for so long, but decided I really wanted to do it again. I trained hard for that fight, but I still lived my life normally. That's when I realized that fighting is second in my life. I ended up beating Gomi, and then the Matt Hughes fight came up. I knew who I was and what I had matured to, and I just remember thinking, "I'm going to walk through him. It's not even going to be a fight." Confidence, huh?

TO: Let's talk about your fights with Renzo and Rodrigo Gracie. Why do you think you can beat guys who have studied the same art, but have studied it twice or three times as long?

BJ: It's about the person you know and it's about what the guy wants to do. I'm not going to say that I took the Renzo fight light, but when it came down to it and the going got tough, who really

wanted to win? I wanted to win and I'm going to win no matter what. I don't care what anyone says, "Oh you look like shit, your fat." Whatever man, I don't care about any of that. I'm not going to let ten minutes in the end of a fight ruin what I've worked so hard for ten years. No way man. It doesn't matter what happens, I'm going to get up, do what I have to do and finish the fight. It doesn't even come down to technique. It's about that right there. (points to heart) It's about doing what you have to do.

TO: If there was anybody in the world that you could fight, who would it be?

BJ: You know, a lot of people ask me that question and I finally know the answer. Even though I get to fight him every day, it's myself. That would be the coolest, to fight an exact replica of myself. I would know what he's going to do, but he would already know what I was going to do. I would just have to out-tough him.

TO: How do you want to be remembered?

BJ: As a guy who never quits.

TO: What are your goals as a coach?

BJ: I was a world champion of BJJ in four years. I've been doing it now for ten years, and only now am I starting to understand it. If there is one thing I can pass on to the guys is an understanding of what jiu-jitsu is all about. When I get older, I'm not going to teach MMA, just BJJ. It's such a beautiful thing in how people learn to move and the laws that come with that.

TO: Hilo is very different than anywhere else in the country and no doubt, you've had a positive influence on a town that needs something positive.

BJ: I'm really outspoken on trying to make something positive because of the drug problem, especially with ICE (crystal methamphetamine).

TO: Anyone you want to thank or anything you would like to say to the fans?

BJ: To all the mixed martial artists out there, all I have to do is watch any one of your fights and I'm a fan of yours instantly. You are the ones that are going to make this the biggest sport. Thanks to all the fans for their support. Aloha! I'd also like to thank my parents, my brothers, my coaches – Rudy Valentino, Charutto, the New Union Team and everybody who has helped me and trained with me along the way.

A KILLER GIVING LIFE

by Adam Villarreal

EL MATADOR TRANSLATED IN ENGLISH MEANS THE KILLING ONE.

Growing up wasn't easy for Roger "El Matador" Huerta. It was something no child or adult should ever experience. His home life was damaged and riddled with abuse from the people who were supposed to care for him most. With an "all or nothing" situation, Huerta never lost hope, once again proving the power of the human spirit.

Born in Los Angeles, but raised in Dallas, Huerta lived with his mother.

"She went kind of crazy and started abusing me when I was little, physically and emotionally.

"My dad got married and my step mom was a crazy lady. She did the same thing to me; she beat on me and abused me emotionally. Finally one day my dad ended up catching her, so he took me to Mexico. He left again and my step mom was like, 'Your dad doesn't live here and I have no responsibility for you,' so she

kicked me out of the house at age 12!" By this time, Huerta was living with a friend, and even though it wasn't the best of circumstances, he was out of physical danger and attended school.

Having a house and having a home are two different things, but Huerta had a hard time understanding the latter. When his senior year rolled around, he met Coach Brian Ashford, who became a mentor showing the teenager all that life

could offer. But something else happened that year. He met Jo Ramirez, who would legally adopt Huerta and become his mother. "She was actually my English teacher and that year, finally everything aligned and my life started to work. She's a mother of seven and all of her kids are successful people, and now they're my brothers and sisters."

No longer looking for a stable roof over his head, Huerta excelled academically and athletically. To this day, he's acquired enough credit to be just two credits away from graduating college. "I was good in spite of how my life was.

"Well I started doing MMA because of my friend Rich Miller. I was doing like 30 second knockouts. I ended up meeting Guy Mezger, and Monte Cox picked me up. He then introduced me to all of his guys."

"It's cool being a Hispanic fighter. A large percentage of pay-per-views come from Hispanics and that's good. I like it. Now the UFC's talking about going to Mexico and I'm thankful they're paying more attention to the Hispanic population. I was proud to be on a card like UFC 69 with so many Hispanic names!" Huerta's fight with Leonard Garcia was the fight of the night. Since September 2004, he has racked up 13 wins, no losses and one no-contest to cement a record of 17-1-1.

"It's motivating and it makes me want the title. My plan is to win the title at 25 (in a year and a half) and then retire with it. My trainer, Justin Hagan, has got me to the point where I never slow down now! Then I want to move to 170 pounds and retire with that, then open up a few gyms. I just want to give back to the community. Sports helped me and kept me disciplined with education. If it can help other individuals, then I want to help and support it."

The Spider Speaks

Translated by
Ed Soares

Interview by
Bobby Pittman

At UFC 64, one of the world's most devastating strikers in the 185-pound division forced his will upon Rich Franklin, then UFC middleweight champ. Though Anderson "The Spider" Silva came in as the underdog, their meeting looked like a mismatch with Silva locking Franklin up in the Thai clinch and battering him with strikes. Just a second short of three minutes, the ref called off the fight and the UFC crowned a new middleweight champion.

MMA WORLDWIDE: Can you describe your childhood?

ANDERSON SILVA: I come from a pretty humble lifestyle and did not have a lot of

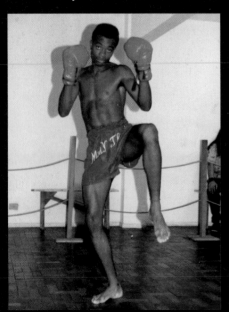

money, but my family taught me a lot of good morals. I was a good-hearted kid. I moved to Curitiba, Brazil at four-years-old to live with my aunt and uncle. I just lived a very simple life.

MW: Describe the differences between living in Brazil and in the US.

AS: The city where I lived in Brazil was very organized and was one of the best cities in Brazil. It was very ahead of its time in transportation. One thing I admire about the USA is that people have a lot of respect for one another in expressing their own identity. People have a lot of respect for one another. Everyone can kind of do their own thing.

MW: When did you discover martial arts?

AS: I basically started training tae kwon do at age seven or eight. My step brother, who is basically my brother, trained Muay Thai, and never let me see him train. One day after leaving school, I walked past the academy

my brother trained at, which was on the way home. I walked by just to watch the people train there and did this three times. On the fourth day, I walked by some of my friends who said they had started training there and said I should too. I started training and it snowballed from there.

MW: When did you realize this is what you wanted to do?

AS: It just kind of happened naturally. When I was growing up doing Muay Thai, I couldn't even afford cable TV. Some of my friends had cable TV and that is how I started watching the UFC and some other events in Brazil that were bare knuckle and some of the first fighting events in the world. I never imagined I would be in this position as the UFC middleweight champion of the world. It just kind of naturally evolved. It wasn't like I had my mind set that this was what I was going to do.

MW: If you weren't doing this, where do

...you see yourself?

AS: I think I would probably be a police officer however, my first job was at McDonald's.

MW: At what age did you start fighting?

AS: About 19 years old.

MW: Were you successful when you first started out?

AS: I have always felt pretty successful. I actually lost my first MMA fight, but like life, that's the way it goes. I am prepared to potentially face losing again. Life does not always work out and success is not always based on whether you win or lose. I feel that success is based on the kind of person you are and the way you treat others. That is how I measure success. My biggest goal is not the journey of wins and losses; I want to come home the same way I left. I want to come back and see my family the same way I left.

MW: What is the worst injury you have had?

AS: I have been very fortunate not to have any very bad injuries, knock on wood.

MW: What is family life like now?

AS: I am married and have four kids, two sons and two daughters.

MW: What are your goals now?

AS: My goal right now is to keep improving and get better and better. I want to work hard towards every fight and give every fight my all. I want to be a good person. I also try to be grateful for the people around me and keep my relationships solid. Being a good person in and outside the ring is most important.

MW: You talk about making friends. Is that your favorite part of fighting?

AS: That definitely is one of the greatest things that comes from doing what I do, but human beings are made to constantly be learning. Every person I have met in my life, whether good or bad at the moment, has made me the man I am. I am constantly trying to improve in every way.

MW: What has been the hardest part with all the changes you've been through?

AS: The worst part of it is having to cut through the rif-raf and finding out who is there for you. It's finding the people who are there to help you. Some people are there to absorb your energy, instead of trying to support it. It's also finding the ass kissers and fakes who maybe just want to be seen with you. I am not the only one that has to deal with this; I am sure every champion has had to deal with that. I don't have any more than Chuck or Fedor or Royce or Minotauro. All these great fighters and champions have had to experience this. The worst part is having to deal with the fake people who just want to benefit from me and not really help me.

MW: What are your plans when you retire?

AS: My dream is just to see my kids grow up and become respectful men and women. Who knows, maybe I'll open a chain of McDonald's (laughs).

MW: Do you see yourself staying in the fight game for the rest of your life?

AS: Definitely having a school is part of my game plan after I retire. I am not really sure if it would be for producing the best fighters in the world, more like producing better people and creating an environment of a martial arts academy. The changes that have happened in my life can hopefully be passed on to my students.

MW: Outside of the fight game, what is your favorite thing to do?

AS: When I can spend the most time with my kids; that is the perfect day.

MW: What is the funniest thing that ever happened while you were training?

AS: I was training with this guy who had his girlfriend there and he was holding the pads. While he was holding the pads, he would keep pulling them down so he could look at his chick, so he wasn't paying attention. When he pulled the pads down again, I was already kicking, so I kicked him in the head and knocked him out. To this day, I will be driving down the street and just think about that and start laughing.

MW: What motivates you to get through the hard times in your career?

AS: Even though we were on opposing teams at one point, the Nogueira brothers and I have always had a good relationship. When I was in a devastating part of my life, when I did not know what I was going to do, they were a very inspirational part of my life. They brought me back into the fighting world and they reassured me. There have been a lot of different people in my life who have helped me a lot, but that had to do with the help the Nogueira brothers gave me.

MW: Anything else you want to add?

AS: I just want to thank all the fans out there who have helped make this sport grow and all the people responsible for helping me get where I am. I am very grateful to the fans. Hopefully they keep watching and the sport keeps growing. The support American fans have given me since I've been here has been great.

In the Bufferzone

by John Stewart

"Let's Get Ready To Rumble®!" You can call it a slogan, you can say it defines boxing, but in reality, it's a brand name that has yielded over $400 million in retail product sales. Bruce Buffer, forever known as the "Voice of the Octagon", took this phrase owned and created by his half brother Michael and turned it into a multi-million dollar empire that includes appearances, licensing deals, videogames, toys and that's just the beginning.

Bruce likes to say, "All business is the same, it's just the product that's different." The business is using the foundation of that famous phrase to span the globe, cross demographics and stay firmly planted in American culture. "It's not about fighting, it's about the will to win…it's the purity of the competitive spirit," says Bruce. "Had it been marketed incorrectly, it would have ended up being another 'Where's the Beef?'. Now it's in its third hour of fame, more popular than ever and my goal is to clear one billion dollars in retail product sales. When I reach that goal, I'll truly be happy."

To learn more about Bruce and Buffer Enterprises, check out his website at www.bufferzone.net.

STITCH

by **Kyle Rayner**

Stitch with Erik Paulson

With all the punches, kicks, knees and elbows, the face becomes an unfortunate canvas for the fighting art. Whether its head lacerations, huge gashes over the eye or nasty arterial cuts, a cutman has less than a minute to apply just enough pressure to keep a fight going. There's a lot at stake. It could be a championship fight with millions on the line or just keeping the fans happy by not having to stop a match prematurely. Whether it's MMA, boxing or kickboxing, there's one name that people trust: Stitch.

Few know him by Jacob Duran, but everyone in the fight game knows 'Stitch'—a man who has dedicated his life to educate people about preventing and stopping cuts and the proper way to wrap hands. You've seen him many times on pay-per-view, presiding over some of the top fighters in the UFC and PrideFC, along with K-1 and boxing. When a fight gets stopped on a cut, every fan gasps in anticipation as Stitch and his fellow cutmen race to keep the fight going, while thinking of the combatant's safety.

Jacob Duran came to work with Alexio at one of his fights when he came across his first case as a cutman. He had learned some of the basics out of necessity, realizing the damage caused by elbows from

Muay Thai. "I didn't know what to do, but knew about applying direct pressure, and he ended up winning the fight."

After that experience, Duran found his calling and picked up his nickname "Stitch", even though he has never stitched up anyone and contends that's not his job.

Duran had known Dana White for years and the UFC President asked him to become part of a trio of cutmen for the organization. "Leon Tabbs, Don House and I are the three amigos; the official cutmen for the UFC," said Stitch.

Stitch says that technique and personality are the two best traits a cutman can have. "A fighter can read you when he's being worked on. Your words of encouragement ease his pain and frustration. When you have 55 seconds to work a cut or prevent one, it means all the difference in the world."

Stitch described three different types of cuts he's worked the most:

GUSHERS

(When the big artery between your eyes running up your forehead is busted.) "It's very difficult to stop these cuts and real-

istically, you're looking at keeping them going for another half round. It's that big artery that pops up when you get excited. During a fight with their hearts pumping so fast, those kinds of cuts open up like faucets." Stitch pointed to the contest between Jay Hieron vs. Jonathan Goulet (Ultimate Fight Night 2) as being the worst cut he's ever worked, but says Edwin Dewees's cut from The Ultimate Fighter Season 4 suffered by Gideon Ray was a close second.

SLICERS

(Deep cuts over/under the eye or cheek.) "These are very severe cuts and happen on a regular basis." In this instance, the cutman uses a cotton swab dipped in epinephrine, along with direct pressure, to close up the blood vessels as much as possible. Avitene is used if the cut is bleeding, while thrombin is used if the blood is removed and the surface is dry.

HAIRY SITUATIONS

(Cuts on the top of the head difficult to find in the hairline.) "I have to say that David Loiseau has given me more work than anyone with those elbows. Stitch also points to the work he did on Elvis Sinosic during his match against Alessio Sakara (UFC 57) as being particularly difficult since Sinosic came into the fight with his hair died red.

Stitch left a lucrative job at RJ Reynolds to become a fulltime cutman. He and his wife Charlotte and their four children (Carla, 28, Angela, 25, Jacob, 22 and Daniel, 12) soon moved to Las Vegas to be closer to the action.

Jacob 'Stitch' Duran will probably work 50 different events in 2007 alone. He's proud of the fact he's wrapped hands for all the top ten heavyweight MMA fighters at one point or another. He's released one documentary and producing another to educate people about how to work cuts, work corners and wrap hands.

When asked what makes him the most proud about being a cutman, Stitch replied: "With every assignment, I've never asked for a job. People always call me for work and I take pride in that." The fans take pride in that too, knowing the best is working to keep their stars in the fight and as safe as possible.

Feel the Rush

by **Adam Villarreal**

UFC President Dana White has called Georges "Rush" St. Pierre the new breed of MMA and fans flocked to the fighter since he first stepped into the Octagon. Within his short career, he has secured victories over every opponent he encountered, save for Matt Hughes; a loss he not only avenged, but took the welterweight title in the process. Unfortunately his reign as champion came to a quick end after suffering an unexpected defeat at the hands of widely-underrated TUF 4 winner Matt "The Terror" Serra at UFC 69.

Even in defeat, the 26-year-old (as of May 19th) was gracious enough to publicly accept his loss and discuss his life outside of fighting, his family, his love life and his plans to get his title back.

MMA WORLDWIDE: How are you feeling since the loss?
GEORGES ST. PIERRE: I'm good. I'm better now. I had a few nights of nightmares, but I'm training and back on track.

MW: How many fights are left on your UFC contract?
GSP: I have five fights left and I don't know who I'm fighting next.

MW: Do you think your heavily-favored odds to defeat Serra affected your performance?
GSP: It's not only that, I had a knee injury, but I had no choice but to fight because I cancelled a fight with Serra before this one.

MW: Tell me about your current family life.
GSP: I still live in my parent's house and I'm about to move out in two weeks.

MW: Tell me about your new house.
GSP: It's not in Montreal; it's a country place. It's in the south shore of Montreal, a big house with four bedrooms.

MW: What did your parents think when you started MMA?
GSP: Well I competed in karate, which was full contact though we weren't allowed to go on the ground and stuff like that. I remember before I did my first amateur fight, they were very worried about me, but then they found out I was good at it, and that I liked what I was doing.

MW: You gave your mother your UFC title belt didn't you?
GSP: Yes, it's at the house right now. I gave it to my mom because she did a lot for me and if it weren't for my mom and dad, I wouldn't have become world champion.

MW: You have a well-documented history with bullies. What would you say now?
GSP: I don't waste my energy hating people. I try to live in a positive way.

MW: What did your parents want you to do for work?
GSP: My parents always told me to do in life what I wanted to do. They kept me in school as long as they could. As an athlete, I train my body, but the most important part of my body to train is my brain.

MW: What was your field of study?
GSP: I studied kinesiology at the university, which is like sports training. I did not finish all my classes, but I have a diploma and I took classes called continuum, but I do plan on getting back to school as soon as possible.

MW: Tell me about your love life.
GSP: I am single right now. I was with a girl for five and half years; she was a very nice girl, a very good person. I think I'm a good person myself, but things didn't work. Since then, I'm single.

MW: What has your success afforded you?
GSP: The most important thing that success gives me is personal satisfaction.

MW: After the UFC 69 press conference, a female asked me what you smelled like. How would you describe your relationship with fans?
GSP: (Laughing) What I smell like? That's pretty odd. I think of the positive things and I use it to motivate me. I have the best fans in the world and I use that kind of stuff as a big motivator.

MW: What is your favorite US city?
GSP: I like Las Vegas and New York because I really know both places very well. My most favorite city is Las Vegas.

MW: Any last words for your fans?
GSP: I just want them to know I'll be back and not to worry about me. I'm more pumped up than ever and I'll be stronger next time!

Whatever happens in St. Pierre's professional future, his confidence is riding high on his newfound drive to get back to the winning ways that put the gold around his waist.

CARLSON GRACIE TEAM

The world of MMA and Brazilian jiu-jitsu suffered a tragic loss, as Grandmaster Carlson Gracie Sr. passed away on February 1, 2007 at the age of 72 in Chicago, Illinois. Kidney and bladder pain forced Gracie to be hospitalized on January 26. Over the next few days, Carlson's condition improved and on the 31st, his heart rate was fine and he had no fever. At 6:00 AM the following morning, however, Carlson passed away when his heart rate dropped sending him into full cardiopulmonary arrest.

Son of Carlos Gracie, founder of Gracie Jiu-Jitsu, Carlson was known by many to be one of the best mixed martial artists of his era. His most famous victories came from facing Waldemar Santana, who had defeated uncle Helio Gracie (at age 43) after battling for more than three hours. At age 17, Carlson defended the family honor and beat Waldemar in just 40 minutes. Carlson rematched him several times, but never lost. Carlson's toughest fight was a draw against Ivan Gomes, arguably one of the best fighters from the day who was not a Gracie. These fights were legendary in Brazil from the mid-1950s through the 1960s.

After his illustrious fighting career came to an end, Carlson graduated to coaching many of today's top fighters and BJJ competitors including Ze Mario Sperry, Wallid Ismail, Vitor Belfort, Murilo Bustamante, Ricardo Liborio, and many more.

Our hearts go out to the Gracie Family and friends of Carlson who suffered from this tragic loss. Carlson Gracie Sr. – You will always remain in our hearts! Rest in Peace.

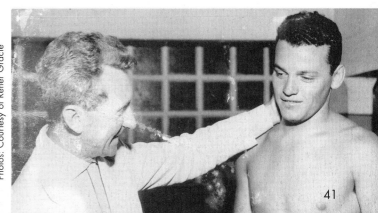

guess the
Cauliflower Ear

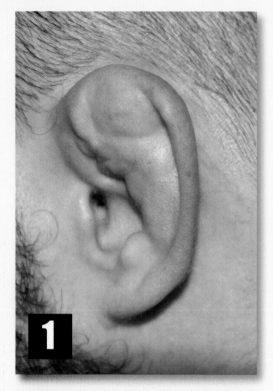

1

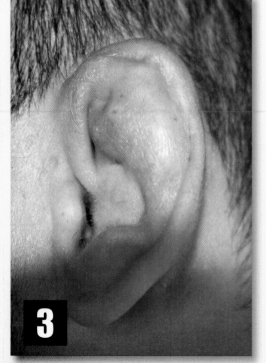

3

Call it a trophy, call it a symbol of strength, call it a rite of passage; whatever you want to call it, the MMA community knows what it is. For those that do not, cauliflower ear occurs when damage afflicts the ear, usually associated with grappling or striking, and swelling occurs. If not drained that swelling hardens and keeps its shape.

This familiar misshapen glob of twisted cartilage lets everyone around you know you have been through your share of battles and is a trademark to many fighters who wear their crowns with pride.

How well do you know MMA ears?

Take your guess as to whose ears these are and check your answers on www.mmaworldwide.com

Good luck!

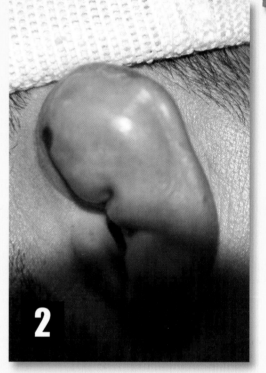

2

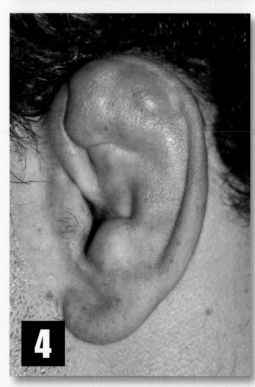

4

10 MOST IMPORTANT MOMENTS IN MMA HISTORY

by Clyde Gentry III

JUNE 26, 1976:
MUHAMMAD ALI
vs. ANTONIO INOKI

Antonio Inoki, one of Japan's all-time greatest pro wrestlers, frequently fought real fighters in stiff-worked matches during the 1970s to put himself over with the crowd. In a match pitting wrestler vs. boxer, Inoki would compete against the biggest name out there: Muhammad Ali. When Ali arrived for the fight, first it was scripted, then it wasn't, then it was 100% legit save for concessions against Inoki, who was not allowed to take Ali down. Over the course of 15 boring rounds, Ali threw a total of six punches, landed two and spent the rest of the time getting kicked in the legs by Inoki. Ali got $1.8 million for his troubles and had to be rushed to the hospital to have blood clots removed from his legs. It was a dark day for boxing, it nearly destroyed pro wrestling in Japan, but it was the first big mixed martial arts fight. "Judo" Gene LeBell served as referee.

SEPTEMBER 1989:
PLAYBOY ARTICLE
CREATES UFC

Entitled "Bad" for the September 1989 issue of *Playboy*, freelance writer Pat Jordan built up the "Gracie Challenge" and brought heated attention to Rorion's Gracie's fledgling Brazilian jiu-jitsu school with scores of wannabe badasses storming to his dojo. This article was indirectly responsible for the creation of the UFC. Ad man Art Davie read the article and befriended Gracie. When the two mapped out a plan for War of the Worlds (which later became the UFC), they sent the article and other materials to production companies. No one was interested. When SEG (Semaphore Entertainment Group) programming director Campbell McLaren came across the article, he found the material compelling and wanted to build off the "Gracie Challenge" to create a pay-per-view spectacle. The Ultimate Fighting Championship debuted November 12, 1993.

FEBRUARY 1995:
INTERNET SAVES A SPORT

Just as no-holds-barred fever was taking off, Canadian George Charylwood created The Fighting List as a way for Internet savvy fans to communicate about the fledgling sport. The Fighting List became The Combat List, an exhaustive e-mail list of hardcores (fans, promoters and fighters) who couldn't get enough of the UFC and the sport in general. When SEG was floundering and the UFC was nixed from pay-per-view, the grassroots Internet campaign kept everyone's hopes alive. In the late 1990s, The New Full

Contact and Full Contact Fighter (website and newspaper) were born and fans were always up to date with the latest information. Eventually www.mma.tv, www.sherdog.com and www.mmaweekly.com joined the pack. One of the sport's most ardent Internet hounds, Joe Silva, had forged a steady relationship with SEG and eventually became the matchmaker for the organization. He is the only remaining member from SEG who works in this capacity for Zuffa's UFC. With the Internet, those years off cable most likely would have seen an end to the UFC before Zuffa even had a chance to buy it.

FEBRUARY 1997:
JUDGEMENT DAY

After a political backlash forced the UFC to move from Niagra Falls to Dothan, Alabama for its twelfth event, SEG staged a meeting with Leo J. Hindery who had become the new president for TCI Cable. Art Davie, Bob Meyrowitz and "Big" John McCarthy met with Hindery, who told them he wanted no part of the UFC or the sport. UFC XIII played to only about 10% of its original pay-per-view universe and that struggle cost SEG millions. The TCI, Time Warner and Viewers Choice ban essentially made MMA obsolete with the mainstream; political pressure died along with it. As a result, however, new rules were instituted and four-ounce gloves would be required for all fighters despite the fact that gloves made the sport more dangerous. New rules typically accompanied each event after that, followed by more weight classes. Ironically, this was good news for the long term because it took the UFC, and most of the other MMA organizations, away from the spectacle to a professional sport with solidarity in rules and regulations.

MARCH 16, 1998:
UNFORTUNATE LOSS

American fighter Douglas Dedge died of brain-related complications after competing in an event held in the Ukraine. "We heard through guys that were with him that he was blacking out during training," said Clarence Thatch, who fought and served as corner man at the event. "As far as refereeing, it was all legit and there was nothing illegal." According to Thatch, the match was stopped after Dedge took six or seven shots to the head. Dedge collapsed after being stood up for the decision and the promotion had no purse money for his wife who had accompanied him. She had to fly back with the body herself. News of this event created a political firestorm, arming MMA opponents with the ammunition they needed all along: the first MMA death. But this time it was former UFC matchmaker Art Davie leading the way; he

made a lot of enemies saying the sport should be banned. Even Stephen Quadros blasted MMA as a sport, long before he became one of MMA's most popular commentators. Dedge was unfortunate, most say it was a pre-existing condition and he was the first and only known fatality known from an MMA fight.

MAY 7, 1999:
ROUNDS

The original attraction to the UFC was anything goes and fight till someone can't fight any longer. But when you're dealing with professional athletes, pay-per-view and judging, you can't take anything for granted. When Bas Rutten fought Kevin Randleman at UFC 20, there was one 10-minute round and two overtimes. Randleman completely dominated the first few minutes and though he stayed top side and damaged Rutten, the Holland super striker kept his composure and drug the fight to a decision. It's hard to say who won the fight, but Rutten was battered, bleeding and had a broken nose while Randleman walked away unscathed. How do you judge a fight without a 10-point must system? Beginning with UFC 21, all non-championship fights are three 5-minute rounds and championship fights are five 5-minute rounds.

JANUARY 9, 2001:
CHANGING OF THE GUARD

On July 17, 1999, the Nevada State Athletic Commission was invited to see UFC 21 for themselves and amongst the group was closet MMA fan Lorenzo Fertitta, who was impressed with the fighters' athleticism. Upon returning to Vegas, he took up training BJJ with John Lewis. When SEG's money problems turned into putting the UFC up for sale, Lewis turned to Fertitta, who along with his brother Frank, could do some big things for the UFC. On January 9, 2001, the Fertittas bought the UFC from Bob Meyrowitz and created a new company called Zuffa (meaning "to fight") Entertainment. Through their connections, they were able to get the UFC licensed in Nevada and lost millions of dollars trying to market the "new" UFC. In the end, Zuffa's UFC has virtually taken over the sport and eaten up its rivals in a quest to keep MMA the fastest growing sport in the world.

SEPTEMBER 28, 2001:
FIRST NIGHT IN SIN CITY

After two shows under the Zuffa banner, UFC 33: Victory in Vegas made headlines, reminded many folks the UFC was still around and for the first time in four years, put the show back on much of the pay-per-view

universe it had lost. With a stacked card featuring Tito Ortiz, Chuck Liddell and Jens Pulver, everyone thought it was a safe bet. Unfortunately things didn't turn out well. Out of eight fights, six ended by decision, and no matter what the live crowd thought, it would be the pay-per-view audience that suffered most. The event ran over its three-hour slot by several minutes and many did not get to see the last round of Ortiz's fight. Thus, pay-per-view buys were out the window as much of the money had to be refunded. While UFC 34 went down as one of the most spectacular shows in recent memory, it took several more shows and The Ultimate Fighter to gain back respectable pay-per-view numbers.

JUNE 25, 2002:
BEST DAMN NEWS

After a guest appearance on *The Best Damn Sports Show Period!*, Bruce Buffer was able to perk the interest of Fox execs into a meeting with the UFC brass. That meeting produced a first for MMA: the airing of one complete fight on free television. Held June 22, the aptly named UFC 37.5 played live to a small crowd as Robbie Lawler, the latest UFC poster boy, faced off against Steve Berger for the televised bout. The fight was solid, it landed the UFC two 30-minute shows on Fox Sports and was the biggest development in the sport's history at the time.

JANUARY 18, 2005:
THE ULTIMATE FIGHTER

When SPIKE TV debuted as the network for men, it was only a matter of time before they would cross paths with the UFC. Given the reality TV craze, the dropping in pay-per-view numbers for pro wrestling and boxing, the UFC was tailor-made for a reality show. The first season showcased two teams taught by Chuck Liddell and Randy Couture respectively, who would compete in challenges and have single fights with each episode. While the team challenges didn't exactly work, the show made Dana White into a major reality star since his no-nonsense, bad guy routine was perfectly suited for the show. As for the fighters, it made superstars out of many of them: Forrest Griffin, Diego Sanchez, Josh Koscheck, Stephan Bonnar and Chris Leben. And with viewers making that personal connection to the fighters, the UFC pay-per-view buys went from 75,000 to 250,000 to 400,000 to over a million just two years later. With free and pay-per-view shows coming almost every two weeks, *The Ultimate Fighter* was the best thing that ever happened to the sport and that's why the series is entering its sixth season with an eighth on the way.

MMA WORLDWIDE

HEAVYWEIGHT 205 AND ABOVE

1	**Fedor Emelianenko**
2	Antonio Rodrigo Nogueira
3	Josh Barnett
4	Randy Couture
5	Gabriel Gonzaga
6	Mirko Filipovic
7	Tim Sylvia
8	Mark Hunt
9	Andrei Arlovski
10	Alexander Emelianenko

Match against Randy becoming more lucrative every day.

Beats Gonzaga and Father Time by TKO in the third round.

Rebound time. Fights Brandon Vera to get back on track.

LIGHT HEAVYWEIGHT 205

1	**Mauricio "Shogun" Rua**
2	Quinton "Rampage" Jackson
3	Dan Henderson
4	Wanderlei Silva
5	Chuck Liddell
6	Rameau Thierry Sokoudjou
7	Antonio Rogerio Nogueira
8	Ricardo Arona
9	Tito Ortiz
10	Rashad Evans

UFC debut against Forrest Griffin September 22nd.

FINALLY! Signs deal to fight in the UFC.

Wins bronze medal in boxing at the Pan American games. No MMA?

Top Ten Rankings

Think your rankings are better? Send us yours at feedback@tapoutmagazine.com

MIDDLEWEIGHT 185

1 **Anderson Silva**

2 Paulo Filho

3 Matt Lindland

4 Dan Henderson

5 Denis Kang

6 Rich Franklin

7 Robbie Lawler

8 Frank Trigg

9 Jason Miller

10 Kazuo Misaki

American debut for Filho successful with 1st round TKO over Joe Doerksen.

Round two, Franklin vs Silva October 20th!

Another fighter lost in Zuffa's purchase of Pride.

WELTERWEIGHT 170

1 **Georges St. Pierre**

2 Matt Hughes

3 Matt Serra

4 Josh Koscheck

5 Jake Shields

6 Diego Sanchez

7 Karo Parisyan

8 Akira Kikuchi

9 Jon Fitch

10 Carlos Condit

Back on the winning track with a "W" over Koscheck.

Back to back wins in GCM.

Gives Brock Larson his second defeat ever in title defense.

LIGHTWEIGHT 160 AND BELOW

1 **Takanori Gomi**

2 Hayato Sakurai

3 Gilbert Melendez

4 Tatsuya Kawajiri

5 Shinya Aoki

6 Sean Sherk

7 BJ Penn

8 Joachim Hansen

9 Vitor "Shaolin" Ribeiro

10 Joe Stevenson

Rumors of a deal with K-1 Heroes will hopefully put Gomi back in action.

Sherk may have to relinquish his belt after positive drug test.

Looked sharp against Kurt Pelligrino. Title shot?

MAIA SUPERSHOW

Martial Arts celebrities shared the spotlight with Bodyguard Magazine during the MAIA (Martial Arts Industry Association) Super Show.

After months of hard work and preparation we finally felt ready! So, on April 30th, 2004 we launched our premier issue. A lot of people put forth all of their effort into the show, so it was really exciting to see it all pay off!

After a seminar to a capacity crowd, Royce Gracie introduced his fans to Robert Pittman, publisher of Bodyguard Magazine. Bodyguard's booth was mobbed when Pittman announced that Gracie and Ron Van Browning would personally autograph copies of the premier issue of the new magazine.

Bodyguard thanks those who helped make the Super Show a success. We met over 20 stars who will also be featured in upcoming issues. We look forward to celebrating our anniversary with you in 2005!

Bodyguard brings smiles to 2 legends!

The Bodyguard booth

Royce instructs an eager crowd

Nikki gives Bodyguard Magazine's success 2 thumbs up!

Frank Shamrock & Bas Rutten with the BG team

Whether smiling or serious, Royce is always ready

Cung Le & Bobby dishing out knuckle sandwiches!

Bob, Bobby & the legendary Bill "Superfoot" Wallace

BATTLE AT THE BELLAGIO II

Royce enjoying the night

Muhammad Ali gets the crowd going

Chuck Liddell & Ron Van Browning

The crowd still loves Mike!

Bob & Don Frye chum it up

David vs. Goliath!

Sheree & Tito Ortiz shoot the breeze

Kimo hangs loose

Bone-crushing kicks and jaw-dropping knockdowns! Bodyguard's staff watched in awe as the kick boxers slammed each other around the ring in the K-1 fights at the Bellagio Hotel in Las Vegas in April.

As we entered, the excitement and fanfare was reverberating through the arena. One of the highlights of the night was hearing the chant, "Ali – Ali – Ali." We were happy to see the winners in the competitions receive their trophies from the hands of the famous Muhammad Ali and Mike Tyson.

We had an opportunity to meet many of the fighters and stars and ask if they would be in our future issues. We were pleased that Chuck Liddell, Bas Rutten, Marcos Ruas, Don Frye, Big John McCarthy, Bill "Superfoot" Wallace, and many others welcomed the opportunity.

Watch for some amazing lessons in the art of kickboxing in upcoming issues of Bodyguard!

Randy "The Natural" Couture needs no introduction as a multi-time UFC champion at heavyweight and light heavyweight. As a four time Greco-Roman wrestling national champion, Randy's takedowns and ground and pound have proven nearly unstoppable in the cage. Now in the UFC hall of fame, Couture stands as the first man ever to hold two major belts in two different weight classes. TapouT Magazine is fortunate to have Randy share with us some of his skills that have made him a living legend.

Guard Pass

Joker has Randy in his full, open guard.

Randy extends his hips forward pushing Joker's legs back and opening his guard fully.

While still extending his hips, Randy pushes Joker's right leg across Joker's left leg.

Randy then settles his hips on top of Joker isolating Joker's right leg and pressing it against the mat. Notice Randy's right knee is on top of Joker's left leg.

With the guard passed, Randy is free to punch with both hands...

...to Joker's dismay.

Joker has Randy in a body lock.

Randy brings his right leg tight against the outside of Joker's left leg.

Randy then brings his right arm around Joker's head and tight against his ear.

Randy then pushes in with his knee and pulls Joker's head down and out, getting Joker off-balance.

Randy then uses the space created to under hook with his left arm.

Randy then hikes up the under hook creating space...

...for a right knee to the body.

Counter to a Thai Clinch

Freddy has Randy in a Thai clinch.

Randy comes around Freddy's head with his left arm and cups across his ear. He grips Freddy's waist with his right hand.

Randy then pulls with his left arm while pushing forward with his left shoulder breaking the clinch. He also pulls in with his right arm.

Here is a closer look at the position.

Randy slides his right arm up from the waist and into an under hook.

Randy then cranks up on the under hook and turns Freddy's hips out.

Randy then steps across with his left foot, drops his level, and prepares to knee tap Freddy.

Randy drives Freddy to the mat by pushing with his under hook and pulling at the knee.

Then quickly gains side mount.

story and photos by Bobby Pittman

There are very few combat athletes in the world who can be recognized solely by their nickname. But when anyone in mixed martial arts around the world hears the name "The Westside Strangler," there is no doubt it is Chris Brennan. A unique breed of athlete, Brennan is a master grappler, no-holds-barred star, and elite submission fighter who not only talks the talk but also walks the walk. Since beginning in Brazilian jiu-jitsu in the early '90s, Brennan has continually honed both his teaching and fighting skills to become an acknowledged master of both. One of the few combat athletes to have competed successfully in UFC, Pride, KOTC, Gladiator Challenge, Extreme Challenge and more, Brennan recently added another feather to his cap when he had the extreme honor of being the first grappler to be given an open invitation to the 2005 ADCC World Submission Wrestling Championships. "Only the best of the best get invited to compete in the ADCC tournament," says Brennan. "So to get that call to compete was a validation of all the time, effort and passion I've put into the sport over the years."

For information on grappling classes at Chris Brennan's Next Generation Fighting Academy, or to inquire about NHB fight training or Chris' worldwide seminar tour, visit http://chrisbrennan.com

High Crotch to Double-Leg Takedown

Chris Brennan is tied up with his brother Jake, with his left hand on Jake's neck and right hand on Jake's left elbow.

Chris releases Jake's neck, shoots for the takedown, and grabs Jake's left leg with his left arm. Notice how Chris uses his right arm to bring Jake's left arm over his head. If he were to let Jake get an underhook he would be thrown to his back.

Chris wraps his right arm around Jake's leg.

Bringing his left arm across, Chris grabs Jake's right leg for a double-leg.

Chris brings his right foot forward and posts it on the ground.

Arching his back, Chris lifts Jake off the ground.

Chris dumps Jake on his back and ends up in side mount. Notice how Chris controls Jake's legs to avoid being put into Jake's guard.

Shawn Chitwood, former world champion, holds multiple black belts and has studied Judo and Jiu-jitsu since 1980. He has trained extensively in Brazilian Jiu-jitsu since 1993. Shawn is a very sought after law enforcement tactical trainer and is the lead law enforcement instructor for the state of Ohio. Craig Chitwood holds a black belt in Jiu-jitsu. As a competitor, Craig has won multiple National Sport Jiu-Jitsu Championships as well as many Brazilian Jiu-Jitsu Championships. Team Chitwood is a proud member of the Saulo Ribeiro Jiu-Jitsu Association. For more information or to purchase their DVDs go to www.teamchitwood.com.

Crawl Armlock from the Mount

Shawn attains the mount position on Craig. Craig wraps Shawn's head to prevent him from rising up and dog paws Shawn's left bicep in an attempt to block incoming punches.

Shawn then circles his left arm over Craig's head placing his elbow by Craig's neck. He uses his right arm to trap Craig's elbow by reaching across for his own left shoulder.

Shawn then drives his elbow back against Craig's head and occupies his defenses with a forearm choke.

Next, Shawn places his head on the ground. He loops his right shin across Craig's stomach by placing his weight on his right knee. Shawn begins to straighten Craig's arm by driving with his body weight.

In this alternate view of the last step, you can see how Shawn has looped his leg across Craig's stomach and how he is straightening the arm.

Shawn now drives his left shin across Craig's neck and releases the forearm choke. When Craig blocks the forearm choke he can't prevent the shin from coming across his neck.

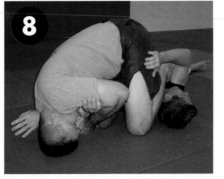

In this alternate view of the last step, you can see Shawn's leg position and how he has crawled across Craig's body.

Shawn stays on his right elbow and ensures that the crook of his right elbow pinches Craig's upper arm. Shawn extends his body slightly driving his right shoulder into the ground and his knees into Craig for the submission.

Neck Crank Defense to Armbar

From the top position in the closed guard, Craig wraps Shawn's head.

Craig stands to apply pressure on the neck crank, also known as the "can opener", to get Shawn to open his legs or to submit.

Shawn then places both his arms, left hand under right, under Craig's chin. It is important for Shawn to lock his arms out and pinch his elbows together so that any pressure applied by Craig is redirected back into his own neck.

Without releasing his closed guard, Shawn under hooks Craig's left leg with his right arm and turns Craig's head with his left arm. Shawn tries to get his head as close to Craig's leg as possible.

Shawn now releases the closed guard, placing his left foot on Craig's hip to drive his hips to a perpendicular angle. At the same time, Shawn bites down with his right leg across Craig's back from his left armpit towards his right.

Shawn keeps his hips in Craig's armpit and swings his left leg over Craig's head, biting down tightly. Shawn uses his left arm to secure Craig's arm and extends his hips while pulling his heels to his butt to finish the arm lock. Shawn maintains his under hook to prevent Craig from picking him up and slamming him back down.

story and photos by Bobby Pittman

With a record of 28-6-2, Pat Miletich "The Croation Sensation" is one of the world's most experienced and respected fighters. The list of his "victims" reads like a Who's Who of MMA fighting and includes such world-class athletes as Shonie Carter, Andre Pederneiras, Jorge Patino, Chris Brennan, and Townsend Saunders. As well known as he is as a fighter, however, Miletich has established an even greater reputation as a trainer and coach for Team Miletich, the single most feared fighting academy in the world, which boasts such stars as Matt Hughes, Robbie Lawler, Tim Sylvia, Jeremy Horn, and others. A competent grappler, Miletich is admittedly most explosive on his feet, where he can deliver punishment with the hands, elbows, knees, or feet. "A complete fighter has to know how to strike," says Miletich. "Grappling specialists just don't last very long in the Octagon anymore."

Left-Hook Block and Counter

LEFT-HOOK BLOCK AND COUNTER

Pat Miletich squares-up with opponent Matt Hughes.

As Hughes throws a left hook, Miletich brings up his right hand to block the punch, like he is combing his hair, while simultaneously turning his body to cock his left hand.

He then counterpunches to Hughes' chin.

Clinch Defense

Pat Miletich is clinched by opponent Matt Hughes.

Miletich steps between Hughes' legs with his left foot, pushes his hips forward, and then straightens his back so Hughes can't pull him down.

Miletich then locks his hands around Hughes' waist and pulls him inward.

Pat then steps behind him with his right foot while keeping his hands locked, and prepares to trip Hughes down.

story and photos by Bobby Pittman

Despite being the world's most famous living martial artist, Royce Gracie has never stopped training and learning in his constant pursuit of excellence.

When Royce Gracie stepped into the Octagon at the first UFC in Denver, Colorado in 1993, he changed martial arts forever. Energizing the entire world with jiu-jitsu techniques that overcame speed, power and size, Royce started a grappling revolution that endures to this day. But from that first UFC until now, Royce Gracie has never stopped training and learning. "My family's jiu-jitsu always incorporated many different styles of fighting," says Royce. "It wasn't just pure jiu-jitsu but also had elements of striking and wrestling. So it only stands to reason that it would continue to evolve. Although the basics that you see today are similar to what I used to win the first UFC, the vale tudo part of the art has evolved since then with more emphasis on no-gi techniques, muay Thai and kickboxing methods, and foot and leg locks. In life, change is part of growth and it should be embraced and not avoided." Here Royce demonstrates some of his favorite moves.

For more information on seminars and training with Royce Gracie, visit www.roycegracie.tv

Shoulder Lock

SHOULDER LOCK

You have your opponent in the mounted position.

Grab his left hand with both of your hands and force it to the mat. His palm should be facing up. Keep your left elbow against your opponent's neck.

Slide your right hand under your opponent's arm and grab your left wrist. Notice how Royce does not grab with his thumbs around the wrist. This will give you a stronger grip.

Put your head on top of your wrists. Pull straight down towards your hips and lift his elbow to finish the shoulder lock.

Your opponent locks his hands around your waist from behind you.

Spread your legs out for base. Lean forward until your hands touch the floor.

Reach in between your legs and grab your opponent's right ankle.

5

Keep lifting his leg until he lets go of your waist and falls backward. Sit down on his knee to finish the knee bar.

Bas "El Guapo" Rutten is one of the most recognizable faces in the MMA world. A former King of Pancrase and UFC champion, Rutten is one of the most respected kick boxers in fighting as well as a very dangerous submission fighter. The Dutch fighter is also one of the most well respected trainers in MMA having coach the likes of Mark Kerr, Duane Ludwig, Genki Sudo and Carlos Newton. He is perhaps most famous for his work out of the ring as an actor and fight announcer as well as the face of the International Fight League.

Bear Hug Escape to Kimura

Your opponent locks his hands around your waist from behind you.

Grab the top of your opponent's right hand with your left hand. Hook your right arm behind his right elbow.

Push against his wrist with your left hand until he lets go.

Now lock the Kimura. Your left hand should be on his right wrist. Your right hand should be holding your left wrist.

Turn into your opponent and force his arm behind his back.

Keep pushing his arm until he leans forward and rolls over.

This is where he should end up.

Let go and take a step back.

Finish with a right kick to the head.

Your opponent shoots in to take you down.

Keep your legs back, and stop his shot with your shoulders and arms. You should have an over hook with your left arm and an under hook with your right arm.

Take a step back with your left foot.

Turn your body and throw your opponent to your left. You should pull with your left arm and push with your right arm.

This is where your opponent should land.

Keep holding his right arm to control him.

Throw a right punch to his face.

Finish with a right stomp to his face.

Boom!

TAKEDOWN DEFENSE

Ken "The World's Most Dangerous Man" Shamrock helped pioneer the sport of MMA as we know it today. A regular in the earliest fights promoted by the UFC and Pancrase, many consider Shamrock the first true mixed martial artist as he combined striking, wrestling and submissions into his fight game early on. Brother to fellow MMA legend Frank Shamrock, Ken is also founder of the Lion's Den, one of MMA's most storied fight teams. This UFC Hall of Famer boasts wins over the likes of Matt Hume, Bas Rutten, Maurice Smith and Dan Severn.

Ankle lock from a left punch

Slip the punch by turning your body to the right (take a small step if needed).

Grab the back of his neck, with his arm still on your left shoulder.

Hang on to his neck as you shoot your right leg between his right leg. Your left leg goes outside of his right leg.

Hook your right leg behind his calf and put your left leg on his right hip.

Wrap your right arm around his ankle and keep it close to your body. Now use your legs and body to force him backwards.

Once he hits the ground lock your legs and apply the heel hook. Hook the foot as shown and lift your right arm straight up.

Neck crank from a two-hand front choke

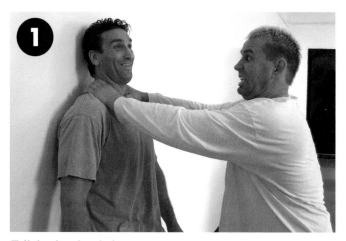

Erik begins the choke.

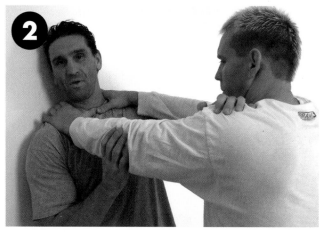

With your left hand go underneath his arms and place your hand on his left shoulder. Bring your right hand to his left elbow.

Lift his arm up and over your head. Make sure you keep your left hand on his left shoulder.

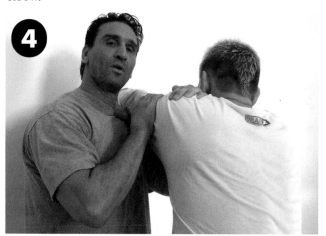

Place his arm on your left shoulder next to your neck.

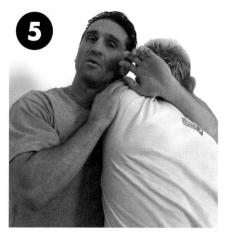

Now hook your left arm around his neck. Use your right hand to push his arm further past your neck, creating a tighter lock.

Grab your right bicep with your left hand. Place your right hand on his forehead.

Squeeze with your left arm, and push away with your right to apply a neck crank.

Mike Swain is hands down America's most accomplished judoka. As a four time Olympian, 5 time national champion and the first American male ever to win a world championship, Mike has made his mark forever in the sport of judo. Currently living in Campbell, California, Mike is also the owner of Swain Mats, a martial arts flooring company specializing in MMA matting. Mike was kind enough to show us some basic judo throws.

For more info log on to www.swainmats.com.

Tio Io-Toshi (Thigh Body Drop)

Mike under hooks Chuck with his left arm. Notice Mike's forehead is in Chuck's temple.

Mike takes a step with his left foot.

Mike then grabs Chuck's left wrist and pivots his hips into Chuck.

Mike brings Chuck's left wrist across his body, drives Chuck's right shoulder down and rotates Chuck's body over his leg...

...throwing Chuck.

Mike maintains his hold on Chuck's left wrist, puts his knee on Chuck's belly...

...and finishes with an arm bar.

Mike has his left hand around the back of Chuck's neck. Notice Mike's head position.

Mike grabs Chuck's left wrist with his right hand while hooking his left heel behind Chuck's left knee.

Mike then takes a hop step with his right foot.

Mike then starts to drive Chuck's head down.

Mike launches Chuck by pulling his head down and elevating his left leg.

Mike then lands on top in head and arm control.

O SOTO-GARI (LEG REAP)

Antonio Rodrigo Nogueira is one of the best Brazilian Jiu Jitsu artists in MMA. Dangerous off his back with an uncanny ability to take punishment from the bottom position have paved the way for Nogueira to submit the likes of Mark Coleman, Dan Henderson and Mirko "Cro Cop" Filipovic in PrideFC. One of the best heavyweights to ever compete in MMA, Nogueira's dramatic come-from-behind submissions have made the Brazilian one of the most popular fighters all over the world.

Oma Plata to Arm Bar

Nogueira has Freddy in his full guard.

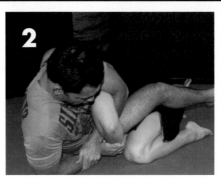

Nogueira goes for a kimura on Freddy's left arm.

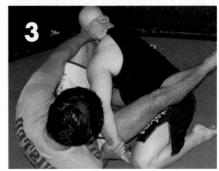

The kimura is used as a set up. Nogueira maintains control of Freddy's left wrist and pushes Freddy's head away with his left hand.

Nogueira then brings his right leg over Freddy's shoulder and bends Freddy's left arm.

Nogueira brings his left leg up to figure 4 Freddy's shoulder.

Nogueira adjusts his grip to...

...straighten Freddy's arm out for an arm bar.

Nogueira posts his right hand on Freddy's leg.

He then rotates his hips across Freddy's elbow and extends his hips finishing the hold.

Anaconda Set Up to Guillotine

1

Nogueira has Freddy in a front head lock.

2

Here is a closer look at his grip.

3

Nogueira brings his elbow in tight, pushing Freddy's arm across.

4

He then attempts an Anaconda choke by grabbing his left forearm with his right hand.

5

Freddy fights his arm out to defend so Nogueira brings his right arm across Freddy's throat.

6

Nogueira grabs his own bicep, puts his left hand on Freddy's shoulder...

7

...and sprawls out his hips finishing the hold.

Carlos Machado is an 8th degree black belt in Brazilian Jiu Jitsu. Having won dozens of titles in BJJ at the state and national level, as well as a Mundials championship, Machado is one of the legendary artists of Brazilian Jiu Jitsu in the world. After moving to the United States in 1990, Machado began his long and successful career as a gym owner and BJJ instructor. Based out of his gym in Dallas, TX, you can find Machado during his long seminar circuit or in one of his many DVDs.

Crossmount Armbar Set Up

Carlos starts with cross face and far elbow control from the right side.

Carlos sets up his right knee on the stomach of his opponent with his left leg posted. His opponent tries to push the knee off his stomach with his left hand.

Carlos grabs with his right arm inside his opponent's left elbow.

Carlos then steps his left leg over his partner's head and maintains tight arm control.

Carlos spins his hip towards the left side and sits on the mat. With his left hand Carlos grabs his opponent's left leg to keep him from rolling. Carlos pulls down with his right hand and raises his hips to finish the armbar.

Rigan Machado began studying Jiu Jitsu as a child in Brazil, training with his cousins, the Gracie family. He was a 3 time National Champion in Brazil and won three Pan American Championships. Rigan was also a medalist at the prestigious Abu-Dhabi World Submission wrestling. He currently operates an academy in Torrance, CA and regularly conducts the "Rigan Machado Camp" where he gathers martial artists from various disciplines for 3 days of intensive training.

He is shown here with Marcos Santos, the Vice President of the Rigan Machado Organization. Marcos owns and operates the Blitz Center Academy in NYC. For info, visit www.blitzcenter.com

Photography by John Ricard. Visit: www.johnricard.com

Closed Guard Pivot to Back Control

From the closed guard, Rigan grabs Marcos' left ankle.

Rigan opens his guard, and begins pivoting towards Marcos' left leg.

Rigan makes a 180 degree pivot and brings both arms behind Marcos' knees.

Rigan escapes his hip to position himself behind Marcos.

Rigan places his shin behind Marcos' knees, while using his left hand to control Marcos' leg. At the same time Rigan holds on to Marcos' belt to prevent Marcos from escaping.

Rigan uses his legs to lift Marcos into the air while pulling down on his belt at the same time.

Rigan keeps his hooks behind Marcos' knees to prevent Marcos from standing. Rigan then begins to apply a lapel choke.

For more info on John, visit www.johnmachado.net.

by Bobby Pittman

John is one of five brothers of the world-renowned Machado Brazilian Jiu-Jitsu martial art family. Born in Rio De Janeiro, Brazil: John began his jiu-jitsu training over twenty years ago. Dominating the competitive arena of Brazilian Jiu-Jitsu in his native country, seizing every major title and competitive award from 1982-1990, John holds the prestigious rank of 4th degree black belt in Brazilian Jiu-Jitsu.

Dominating the Brazilian Jiu-Jitsu scene both in the U.S. and in international competition, John is one of the most admired and respected Brazilian Jiu-Jitsu practitioners in the world today. Recognized and respected for his outstanding fighting and competitive accomplishments, as well as his teaching expertise, John is in demand throughout the world as one of the foremost authorities in the martial arts. John's talent has been showcased in several major motion pictures and television appearances.

Defense to Single Leg

John is standing over his opponent, who has open guard. John steps in between his opponent's legs with his right leg. He uses his hands to control his opponent's legs.

John's opponent sits up and grabs John's right leg with his left arm, to go for the single leg takedown.

John swings his left leg backwards towards his opponent's left side.

Now John sits back and traps his opponent's left leg with his left arm. Notice how John holds his opponent's head up with his right arm for control.

John continues to roll back bringing his opponent flat on his back. He also continues to pull his opponent's left leg up.

Here you can see how John pulls the left leg up for the knee bar.

John locks his hands around his opponent's left leg. His right foot hooks under his opponent's right leg and he arches his hips and applies pressure to the knee bar.

The 2nd oldest son of Helio Gracie, Relson Gracie moved to Hawaii in 1988. He began learning jiu-jitsu at age 2 and entered his first competition at the tender age of 10! He was the Brazilian National Champion for 22 years straight, and during this period went undefeated. He became so popular that he attained the nickname "Campeao" or "Champion" among his friends and fans. Upon his arrival to Honolulu, it was with great pleasure that Relson introduced the art of Gracie Jiu-jitsu to the Aloha State. Now retired from competition, Relson continues to enjoy teaching classes in Hawaii and has become quite fond of the island life. For more info on Relson and how you can train with him, visit www.relsongracie.com.

Arm Bar from the Guard

Relson Gracie has Imiola Lindsey in his open guard. Relson has his right hand inside the collar and his left hand grabs the back of Imiola's right arm. Relson keeps his left foot on Imiola's hip and he uses his right foot to block Imiola from striking with his left hand.

Imiola stands up to try and pass the guard.

Notice how Relson keeps his right foot against Imiola's left arm in case he tries to punch.

Now, Relson puts both feet on Imiola's hips.

Relson pulls Imiola's torso down with his arms and pushes Imiola's hips up with his legs.

Here you can see how Relson elevates Imiola.

Once Imiola is elevated, Relson brings his left leg out and swings it around Imiola's head, letting him fall into an arm bar. Notice how Relson keeps his right foot on Imiola's hip. This is crucial to making Imiola fall into the arm bar.

Imiola lands flat on his back in an arm bar.

Relson squeezes his legs together and raises his hip to finish the arm bar. Relson also makes sure that Imiola's thumb is pointing up to make the arm bar more effective.

Erik Paulson is one of the founding fathers of American Shoot Wrestling. Having studied martial arts in Japan, Paulson turned his love of combat into one of the earliest successful MMA careers for an American. Fighting as early as 1993, Paulson's complete game and dangerous leg locks have made him one of the most sought after coaches in the sport. Having trained the likes of Josh Barnett, Justin Levens and Cub Swanson, Paulson has proven his lessons are invaluable to a fighter.

Opponent is Defending Against You on the Ground

Keep your hands out to protect you from any up kicks. Knees bent to avoid injury if he kicks the legs.

Step inside your opponent's legs, trapping his left leg with your right shin.

Grab his right foot with your left hand, just above his toes.

Fake a punch to get his hands back up and away from his foot.

Slide your right hand behind his foot and grab your left wrist.

Roll onto your right shoulder while keeping the foot lock. Your right foot needs to stay hooked under his left leg.

Use your right leg to pull his leg and turn him over. Also apply the ankle lock. The pain will help him go where you want.

This is how you should finish the roll. You still have the ankle lock secure, and his left leg hooked.

Hook your right foot behind your left knee. Now apply the ankle lock while rolling into your opponent.

Opponent Shoots in, Trying to Grab Your Waist or Leg With His Right Arm

1 Get in a good stance with your hands up.

2 As your opponent shoots in block with your forearm on his shoulder, next to his neck. Use your weight to slow down his momentum. Grab his right wrist with your left hand.

3 Reach over the back of his right arm with your right arm and grab your left wrist.

4 Sit straight back, using your legs to chop his legs down and take away his base.

5 Bring your left leg up onto his lower back to hold him down. Apply the shoulder lock by pushing his arm up and behind his back.

Freddy "Detroit Diesel" George is one of the most dedicated MMA trainers in the game as well as an accomplished strength and conditioning coach. George has trained with some of the sports biggest stars including Ken Shamrock, Quinton "Rampage" Jackson, Josh Barnett, Sean Sherk, and many more. Most of these fighters have come to CSW (Combat Submission Wrestling) where he and Erik Paulson run one of the most talented schools in MMA. An encyclopedia of moves, George has a technique for every position on the mat, ring or cage.

Defending the Takedown Against a Wall (Option 1)

Jay Martinez has Freddy up against the wall and he is trying to take him down with a double leg.

Freddy cross-faces with his right arm, making sure his forearm goes across Jay's jaw line.

Here you can see how Freddy goes for the cross-face. Also notice how Freddy has his left hand on Jay's right shoulder.

In one movement, Freddy lifts with his right arm and pushes down with his left arm, spinning Jay around. Remember: Turn the head and the body will follow.

Here you can see how Freddy spins Jay around.

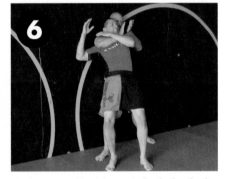

As soon as Freddy gets Jay's back, he drops his right forearm under Jay's chin for the choke, and locks his hands together.

With his hands locked, Freddy starts to drop down by bending his legs.

Here you can see how Freddy drops down and pulls Jay backwards. Notice how Freddy keeps Jay tight against his chest.

Now, Freddy squeezes for the choke.

Defending the Takedown Against a Wall (Option 2)

1

Craig has Freddy up against the wall and he is trying to take him down with a double leg. Freddy immediately gets an under hook with his right arm.

2

Now, Freddy gets an under hook with his left arm and lifts with both arms to peel Craig's hands off his legs. Notice how Freddy keeps his upper body leaning slightly forward to keep Craig's head down.

3

Freddy locks his hands together behind Craig's back.

4

Freddy steps over Craig with his right leg to go into the mount.

5

Here you can see how Freddy steps into the mount.

6

Now, Freddy drops down for the crucifix. Notice, that Freddy never unlocks his hands.

7

Here you can see Freddy's position from another angle. Freddy arches his back and squeezes his arms together to finish the submission.

8

Once Freddy gets to this position he also has another option for the crucifix.

9

This time, instead of stepping over Craig, Freddy steps to the side, bringing Craig to his back.

10

Here you can see how Freddy brings Craig down.

11

Now, Freddy kicks his right leg through (sits out), and sits back to finish the submissions.

Like many, Javier Vazquez began his training in high school, where he started wrestling at age 15. Unlike many, Javier went on to become one of the most talented fighters and trainers in the world. Since he started training BJJ with Rodrigo Medeiros, Javier has earned the rank of black belt and won numerous tournaments across the globe. Javier was also one of the founding members of Millennia Jiu-Jitsu alongside Romie Aram and John Jensen. Now, Javier is teaching at the Javier Jiu-Jitsu Academy in La Habra, CA and if you ever get the chance you should check it out. For more info on Javier and how to train with him, go to www.showtimejiujitsu.com and be sure to check out Javier's DVDs on Mastering Grappling.

Getting the Hooks In from Rear Mount

Javier has the rear mount on Charles. Javier's left knee is on the ground next to Charles' right knee and Javier's right foot is up. Javier locks his arms around Charles' head and left arm.

Keeping his arms locked, Javier rolls onto his left shoulder and pulls Charles over.

Javier continues to roll until he ends up on his back. Notice how Javier kept Charles' body tight against his chest throughout the entire roll.

Once they finish the roll, Javier throws his right leg inside Charles' right leg (right hook in).

Here is another angle of position 4. Notice that Javier has his right hook in and still has his arms locked around Charles' head and arm.

Now, Javier posts his head on the ground and comes up onto his left knee.

Here you can see how Javier is now on his left knee.

Javier rolls to his right side, pulling Charles with him.

Here you can see how Javier rolls to the right.

Javier continues to roll until he can bring his left leg through.

Now, Javier throws his left hook in. Both hooks are now in and Javier can go for the choke with his arms while still controlling Charles with his legs.

Guard Pass to Darse Choke

Javier is in Charles' open guard.

Javier reaches under Charles' left leg to go for the pass.

Javier begins to stack Charles' leg up. Notice what Javier is doing with his arms here. With his right arm, he pushes down on Charles' body. With his left arm, he pushes down on Charles' right leg. This will help keep your opponent from scrambling and putting you back into his guard.

As Javier circles around to pass the guard, Charles blocks his hip with his left hand.

Javier drops his left hip to the mat as he kicks his left leg through, bringing his knee toward Charles' head. At the same time, Javier wraps his right arm around Charles' neck. Notice how Javier's chest coming down pushed Charles' left leg down.

Now, Javier steps over with his right leg.

Here you can see the direction that Javier stepped with his right leg. Javier also wraps his right arm tighter around Charles' neck here.

Javier continues to circle around and also keep his weight down on Charles. With his right hand, Javier grabs his left bicep, locking in the Darse choke (also known as reverse arm triangle).

Javier drops his weight down and squeezes for the submission.

UFC veteran and IFL coach, Matt Lindland is a one of the most decorated wrestlers in MMA today. A silver medalist at the 2000 Olympics, he has dazzled MMA fans with his takedowns and slippery ground work. As one of the founding members of Team Quest in Gresham, Oregon, Matt is currently the head coach of the IFL's Portland Wolfpack. Matt was kind enough to take time out of his busy schedule to show us some of the moves that have carried his career. To learn about Matt and Team Quest log on to www.tqfc.com.

Near-Side Kimura to Switch From Half-Guard

NEAR-SIDE KIMURA TO SWITCH FROM HALF-GUARD

Matt (bottom) has Fred in his half guard.

Matt uses his left forearm to push into Fred's neck to create space.

Matt extends his arm to push Fred's weight off him and get his hips off to the side. Notice Fred's right arm is still around Matt.

Matt controls Fred's right wrist tight against his body.

Matt brings his right arm over Fred's right arm and grabs his left wrist locking up the kimura.

Because Fred defends by grabbing his own thigh, Matt releases the kimura and posts his left hand on the mat so he can scoot his hips out.

Matt grabs Fred's hamstring with his right hand trapping Fred's right arm preparing to switch. Notice how Matt's rear is square on the mat and he is no longer on his hips.

Matt then brings his left arm around Fred's waist and pushes off his left foot to come around Fred's back...

...and finishes on top. Matt can finish with strikes or a choke.

Fred and Matt are squared off.

Fred shoots a single leg on Matt.

Here is a close up on how Matt defends. He has a whizzer (an over hook around Fred's left arm), and grabs Fred's right wrist while keeping his elevated right leg on Fred's left hip.

Matt brings his left leg in close to bait Fred into finishing with a double leg takedown.

Matt uses Fred's momentum and uses his hips and the over hook to slam Fred's head into the ground. Notice how Matt's hips are off to the side.

Matt brings his left arm around Fred's neck to attempt a guillotine.

To keep Fred's arm out of the guillotine and make the choke tighter, Matt stretches Fred out by pushing Fred's left hip with his right foot making space for Matt to bring his right hand in.

Matt then locks his hands together going for the choke while bringing his right leg over Fred's body and squeezing his legs together. Notice how Matt blocks Fred from circling by blocking him with his right shin.

Here is the choke from the original angle.

If not for his bottomless cache of moves, Mike "Joker" Guymon might not have been known for his skills in the ring because of his antics out of it. One of the most engaging personalities in the sport, Guymon has attracted throngs of fans to the sport with his humor and wit. Having competed extensively in King of the Cage as well as the IFL, Guymon is one of the most beloved fighters in the sport. Currently teaching the next class of fighters at Joker's Wild Fighting Academy, Guymon has flourished in his new role as trainer and coach.

Snake Submission from the Mount (bottom)

Andre has the mount on Mike.

Mike goes for the elbow escape on his right side, using his right arm to push Andre's leg away from his body.

Mike brings his right leg out and wraps it around Andre's left leg.

Mike rolls to his left side and traps Andre's right arm. Mike reaches over the arm with his left arm and under it with his right arm.

Here you can see how Mike locks his hands to trap Andre's arm. Notice that Mike's right arm stays above Andre's elbow.

Mike squeezes his arms together, like a scissors motion, pinching Andre's triceps and biceps in between his forearms for the submission.

Defending Ground and Pound Against a Wall

Andre is in Mike's open guard and has him against the wall. From here, Andre is in great position for ground and pound.

Mike uses his hands to block Andre's strikes. Notice how Mike also pushes his hips straight up to keep the distance.

Mike turns his body to the right and wraps his right arm around Andre's left leg. He uses this hook to pull himself through Andre's legs or "out the back door."

Here you can see how Mike pulled himself through Andre's legs.

Now, Mike pushes himself away from Andre so there is space for Andre to fall in front of him.

Mike reaches under Andre's arms and locks his hands together.

Once his hands are locked, Mike pulls Andre backwards. Notice, how Mike uses his legs to control Andre's.

Now, Mike throws both hooks in for even more control. From here he can go for the choke.

Hurb Dean, Chuck Liddell and Freddy George.

Bas Rutten gets adjusted by Dr. Pete.

Wayne Newton joins the crowd for the UFC.

Freddy George and Quinton Jackson get harrassed by a fighter.

"Rampage" Jackson in the gym.

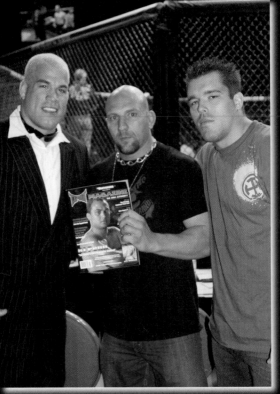
Tito Ortiz, Freddy George and Dean Lister.

Wallid Ismael & Quinton Jackson at a fitness

Kid Rock, Rob Duyrdek and bodyguards.

Tanner Pittman with the beautiful WFA girls.

Tito Ortiz and son Jacob.

Sam Hogar, Hurb Dean, Stephan Quadros, Joe Stevenson, Larry Landless and Javier Vazquez.

"The Pittbull" Andrei Arlovski.

Mario Lopez, the new EliteXC commentator.

Just another day for the TapouT Crew.

Eat to Win

by **Randy Couture**

Over the past two years there has been a lot of interest in the nutritional program I used to come down from the Heavyweight division and compete in the Light Heavyweight division. A special thanks to Joe Rogan for bringing it up in the UFC 44 vs. Tito Ortiz fight broadcast.

Although most folks never have to fight in a cage for 25 minutes, they can use these same principles to enhance the quality of their lives by improving endurance, performance and health. It is well known that certain foods have either an acid or alkaline effect on the body. Animal products, sugar, dairy and processed grains are all acid-forming foods, while vegetables, especially green leafy vegetables, are alkaline. Since the stress of training is also acid-forming, my primary goal is to reduce the amount of acid build-up in my body.

Our bodies regulate the pH of our blood and tissues closer than it regulates body temperature. We must maintain a slightly alkaline pH to survive. Hard training, stress, high protein or high sugar diets can cause acid build-up. While there are mechanisms in place to deal with this acid (it's a natural metabolic by-product), when there is an overload, peak performance and health will often suffer.

I focus on three main areas for my fights. The first is to increase the amount of energy by eating rich live foods. In Las Vegas I usually make a nightly trip to Whole Foods and make sure I continue that right up to fight night. After making weight, I have a large green drink and lots of raw spinach and other greens. The second is to decrease the amount of acid-forming foods while making sure I am still getting all the nutrients I need. This includes reducing red meat and chicken, and eating more fish, almonds and beans. All dairy products are eliminated as well. The third component is proper nutritional supplementation. For example, I eliminated one of my carbohydrate replacement drinks and a few types of energy bars due to their high sugar content. Light Force greens are used daily along with some flaxseed oil.

By including more alkaline foods into my diet and reducing acid forming foods, I feel better and experience more energy. Believe it or not, I did not get tired at all in my five round fight with Tito. This is a testament not only to proper nutrition but also to under-standing and applying the correct training principles so I was able to peak at the right time.

My everyday diet includes green vegetables with each meal. Almost every morning begins with fresh vegetables and an alkalizing Light Force green drink. Grilled fish, soba noodles, high energy pancakes, shots of fresh wheat grass, and fresh vegetables and avocados on yeast free toast are also on the menu. Here are a few things to try:

1. Several times a week, start your day with fresh or lightly steamed vegetables such as cucumber, broccoli, green peppers, spinach, kale, et cetera. Eat again when you get hungry or at least include greens with whatever you're going to eat for breakfast. I prefer to spread hummus on my veggies to help them go down better.

2. Reduce the amount of red meat and poultry. If you do want to eat them, get them from an organic source. There are some great books written on how unhealthy the meat is in the U.S. Don't sweat the protein issue, you need a lot less than you think. Eat almonds (which are very alkaline) and other nuts, seeds, and fish.

3. Drink lots of water. You may need to drink around a gallon a day. Everyone is different and it depends on a number of factors from training to temperature.

4. Include water-rich live foods with each meal.

5. Eliminate as much sugar from your diet as possible. Read labels, you'd be surprised where you'll find it. Soda is a major source and may hurt your conditioning.

6. Add an alkalizing greens supplement to your water a few times a day. I use Light Force which is for sale at www.randy-couture.tv or www.tqfc.com.

This is my nutritional program in a nutshell (no pun intended)! I try to maintain this better than 80 percent of the time, and it gets especially strict in the peaking phase 10 weeks before a fight.

MUSCLE MYTHS

by **Randy Couture**

Photo: Marcel Aniceto

One of the biggest myths I find in our sport is that people think it requires huge amounts of strength to be competitive. I'm not talking about perceptions from the general public who misunderstand us in many ways, I'm referring to athletes in MMA who seem to be under the impression that huge "beach muscles" and being able to bench press 500 lbs. are going to help win more fights. In most cases, in fact, I believe that type of physique and training are counterproductive to MMA success.

Our sport is very unique in its athletic requirements. A good aerobic base is necessary, particularly when a fight can last upwards of 25 minutes. Flexibility is also important as we regularly get put into positions that twist us to the point of extreme contortion. Speed and quick reactions are also key components. Strength is also a nice thing to possess when we are trying to apply a technique, control a position, or land an effective blow. We each possess a combination of these attributes that make us the athlete and fighter that we are. While I do believe there is no substitute for horsepower to effectively execute a learned technique, sport-specific training allows us to take advantage of our physical gifts and attributes. I will give you my philosophy on sport-specific strength training, and then in my future articles discuss the other pieces to the puzzle that make MMA athletes like ourselves unique.

My goal as a fighter is to be able to punch you in the head just as hard in the fifth round as I did in the first. It requires a particular type of strength training to achieve that goal. A common question I get is, "How much do you bench?" My answer? "Who cares!" Much more important is how many repetitions I can do! My ability to bench 300 or 400 pounds only becomes important if I weigh 300 or 400 pounds and am competing against another athlete of that weight. However, there are not many athletes in our sport that heavy. The reality of generating that kind of power requires training with very heavy weights and performing low repetitions. Let's face it, most normal

athletes are not going to push 300 or 400 pounds more than a couple of times. Although it only takes one solid punch to end a fight, we rarely see it. More than likely, we will throw many punches to finish a fight. Therefore, our strength program should simulate and support our most common fight scenarios. That requires higher reps with less weight so you have the strength to throw as many technically proficient, powerful punches as necessary to win a fight.

Now here is the kicker and what I think is misunderstood: high reps with low weight doesn't mean you won't be as strong. On the contrary, I believe you can become stronger with this approach to strength training. Let's take just the typical bench workout for a heavy lifter: He does a warm up set with 225 lbs. for 10 reps, giving him a total moved weight of 2250 lbs. He then does an intermediate set of 275 lbs for 5 reps for a total of 1375 lbs moved. Next a working set of 315 lbs for 3 reps, 945 lbs moved, and a peak set of 350 lbs for 1 rep max; so add 350 lbs to his total for a moved weight of 4920 lbs. Most heavy lifters take lots of rest between sets to allow themselves to get all their reps, so let's estimate a workout time of 25 minutes. So the heavy bencher moved 4920 lbs in 25 minutes.

Now let's lighten the load and increase the reps to simulate a fight. We'll take 125 lbs – easy, right? We're going to do 6 sets which will include a warm-up set and 5 sets to simulate a 5 round fight. We're going to take a 1 minute rest between sets, just like the rest period between rounds, and we're going to do 8 reps each round. If you do the math, the total weight moved is 6000 lbs. I figure 8 reps can be performed pretty easily in 30 seconds time with a 1 minute rest period to recover, for total benching time of 9 minutes. You just moved 6000 lbs in 9 minutes versus 4920 lbs in 25 minutes. So who is stronger? More importantly, which athlete is going to have more endurance (anaerobic capacity) when the fight goes 25 minutes. I think you can see my point.

MUSCLE MYTHS II

by **Randy Couture**

Let's apply the philosophy of more weight in less time to a training plan. You need to work several major muscle groups in a series of sport specific movements to have a complete strength program. It's no different than a bodybuilder working all the muscle groups for size and symmetry; it's just that our goal is different. We want endurance and durability. Most trainers will tell you to only work a muscle group two times per week, so in the program we'll do high reps with low weight through the selected movements twice per week. Rest is also very important for making gains and allowing the body to recuperate. So we'll allow two days of rest before we repeat the training again. Here's a sample workout that incorporates everything we've just discussed. It's a grappling and MMA training circuit, and it's designed with movements that work muscle groups important to our sport.

Grappling/MMA Circuit – Day 1

Set 1: Start with 105 lbs barbells. Do 8 reps for each of following exercises: Bent over rows, Upright rows; Military Press; Good Mornings; Split squat-left; Split squat-right; Squat/push press; Straight leg dead lift. Rest for 60 seconds.

Set 2: Add 10 lbs to each side of bar (125 lbs) and repeat

Set 3: Add 5 lbs to each side (135 lbs) and repeat

Set 4: Same weight as set 3 (135 lbs).

Set 5: Remove 5 lbs each side (125 lbs)

Set 6: Remove 10 lbs each side (105 lbs)

Grappling/MMA Circuit – Day 2
Repeat Day 1

Let's do the math. You've just moved 46,720 lbs in approximately 20 minutes! Take two days rest from lifting and then repeat this total body grappling circuit. Make sure you focus on your form and keep a total running time for your workout. You will see your body adapt to the workload. You will move 46,720 lbs in less and less time. The reps and sets will get easier as you progress, so add more weight. You will get stronger, have more endurance, and be more durable. When I refer to "durability" I mean the ability to avoid injury to joints and muscle tissue. You will also recover faster if you do sustain an injury.

The first thing that happened when I went to the gym to do this circuit was that all the metal-heads looked at my 105 lb. barbell and snickered to themselves. (Not to my face. They weren't stupid!) They watched me go through the routine and saw the sweat puddle on the floor. They finally became curious and so I offered to put one guy through the grappling circuit routine. He did fine until the end of set #4, at which time he promptly dropped the bar and ran to the trashcan to puke! Guess who was snickering to themselves then? (I'm not stupid either!).

This low weight and high rep workout with little rest is very tough. It simulates round length and fight recovery time and works the performance muscle groups for MMA and grappling. Give it a try for 8 to 10 weeks. It's especially good for peaking for a competition. Lifting two days a week instead of the normal four or six days will also free up more time to develop and refine your techniques. You can focus on other facets of the athletic puzzle that makes a well-rounded fighter.

Cutting Weight

by **Randy Couture**

Photo: Marcel Aniceto

There is a right and a wrong way to do anything. Spending most of my life competing in a weight class sport, I've experienced the right and wrong ways to make weight. If you don't want a minute feeling like an hour, don't make the same mistakes I've made. My first weight-cutting experience came in high school sophomore year. I weighed 135 lbs. and was up against a tough senior to make varsity. After losing in a challenge match, I went down to 129 lbs. and challenged for the varsity spot there. Never having cut weight before, I asked the upperclassmen how to do it. Some guys wore sweats under the mats to lose water. Some guys ran in plastic garbage bags to increase their core temperature and sweat rate. Some guys spit the weight off. Most used a combination of these techniques. After spending a sleepless night in my ski clothes and a sleeping bag, then spitting in a cup all day I made weight and won the varsity spot.

Losing 6 lbs. in a day sounds like a lot, but this is just temporary. Seventy percent of your body is made up of water and you fluctuate a few pounds daily. This has no effect on your body composition, body fat, or lean muscle mass. Years later at the Olympic Festival, I was wrestling in the 180.5 lbs. class for the U.S. Army and my walkaround weight was 198. After five days of no food, only fruit, and three days of no water I made weight. I don't think I could have wrestled my way out of a wet paper bag. Consequently, I didn't make weight for the second day of the tournament, and was eliminated. It was a less than stellar performance but I learned a valuable lesson.

Evaluate your body honestly. Get your body-fat tested, determine a realistic weight, and give yourself time to reach that weight. You shouldn't lose more than 4 lbs. of real weight (not water) per week. There is no magic potion or secret formula. Burn more calories than you're putting in, and make sure the calories you do take-in are good ones. Stay hydrated until the last possible moment. This is a science that takes practice. I know once I start sweating, if I keep my core temperature up and keep moving, I will lose 1 lb. every 10 minutes. So if weigh-ins are at 5pm and I am 10 lbs. over, I need at least 15 minutes to break a sweat, then another 90 to 100 minutes to lose that water weight. So allowing travel time to and from the gym and the weigh-ins, I start my weight cut at 2 pm. You can standardize how long it takes to lose a set amount of water by wearing the same gear every time you cut.

You'll need a thick beanie and knit gloves (because you lose body heat from your head and hands), and a good pair of plastic sweats – Fairtex makes a good set! A good cotton layer under your plastics (long johns are perfect) are great, as these soak-up sweat so your body keeps perspiring to cool itself. You'll also need a good cover layer over your plastics to insulate your body and keep your core temperature up. I like heavy cloth sweatpants, because as the sweat moves up my leg I've learned to gauge how much weight I've lost! Once you're dressed, jog or walk on the treadmill and keep yourself moving. If you're 170 lbs. or less I don't recommend losing more than 6-8 lbs. of water to make weight. Over 170 lbs, 10-12 lbs. is workable. A sauna is a last resort. Cut too much and you risk affecting your physical ability to perform.

Rehydration is very important. Slow and steady is the key. Try not to make it too cold or it can upset your stomach. There's nothing worse than puking when you're dying of thirst. Pedialite is the best drink I've found for oral hydration. It's used for rehydrating sick babies and can be found at any grocery store. I don't advocate extreme weight cutting or weight cutting at all for adolescents. Pick a realistic weight and work on your technique. You either have it or you don't, no matter how big or small you are! Do it the right way!

THE 7 GREATEST MYTHS OF COACHING

by **Randy Couture**

We can all name great coaches and we have all been exposed to some not-so-great ones as well. But have you ever thought about what makes a coach great? Many think that if you played a sport that you are qualified to coach it – WRONG! I fly a lot, but I don't think any of you want me to be your pilot on your next vacation! I have a friend who had heart surgery recently and the doctor said that he was an ideal patient – but I don't want my friend operating on me! I think you get my point. Great coaches are made not born. "If you've competed in your sport, then you're qualified to coach it," is simply one of the many myths of coaching. I'm going to explore seven of these myths. Through understanding them, it will help to show that anyone can be a great coach if they are willing to work at it correctly – whether it is at an elite level, a beginner level, or somewhere in-between.

Myth 1: *Winning is everything.*

Winning is not everything, but striving to win, preparing to compete, and employing skills and tactics necessary to win is. Other invaluable coaching skills include knowing how to compete, competing with intensity, and knowing and using the rules. But most important is the athletes overall development including character and attitude. Our spot can be a vehicle for training people to be successful in any endeavor in life.

Myth 2: *If you competed in a sport then you're qualified to coach it.*

I touched on this already. Someone is qualified to coach only after learning the correct principles of coaching and applying them. I've known great coaches who never competed in anything.

Myth 3: *The more titles you won, the better qualified you are to coach.*

In reality, some great athletes make lousy coaches. Athletic ability doesn't necessarily translate into good coaching skills. I've met plenty of great athletes who have no idea how they do what they do – let alone have any clue how to teach it to someone else.

Myth 4: *A male coach is superior to a female coach.*

Any person who has a desire to learn and practices sound coaching habits can succeed as a coach. Coaching skills aren't gender related.

Myth 5: *The more years you have as a coach the better you are at coaching.*

If coaches aren't grounded in good coaching principles and don't continue to learn, their experience will not translate into superior coaching. Good coaches use their experience to deepen and expand their coaching philosophy, technique and skill. Some coaches have 20 years of experience, while other coaches have one year of experience 20 times.

Myth 6: *The best coach is a strict disciplinarian.*

A strict disciplinarian can be a good coach, but a great coach is knowledgeable about the sport, listens to the athletes, understands and responds to their needs, gives them a sense of self worth, and helps them develop and enjoy what they do.

Myth 7: *Trained coaches are needed more at the advanced level, rather than the beginning.*

When you build a house, you don't save the skilled workers for the second floor and use amateurs to lay the foundation. Skilled and knowledgeable coaches for beginners create a fulfilling experience and lay their foundation for future success in sport and in life.

Exploiting these myths and exposing them for what they are will help to educate coaches about what it takes to be truly great. This will now only raise performance in our athletes but elevate our sport in general. It is our responsibility as athletes and coaches to ensure this!

PEAKING PHASE:
When the Rubber Meets the Road

by **Randy Couture**

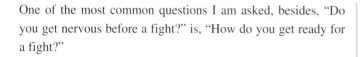

One of the most common questions I am asked, besides, "Do you get nervous before a fight?" is, "How do you get ready for a fight?"

One primary key to my success and longevity in MMA relies on maintaining a high fitness base. Now I wasn't always this way. I was like a bulimic at a buffet as a young athlete. Binge and purge, binge and purge; actually it was more like train, compete and either celebrate, or commiserate depending on performance, then show up, get in shape and do it all again.

Fortunately we get smarter with age and experience. I learned it was easier to stay in shape between competitions rather than go through aches, pains and suffering to get back in shape to perform. I found I was injured less; my peak performances were more successful.

In wrestling I competed a lot during a season or throughout the year. It would be crazy to think every performance in that environment could be at peak. I would therefore pick two or three competitions in the year that had significance to me, focusing my training plans to peak for those events.

Transitioning to MMA, I applied the same theory to having the best performances in my fights. I came up with a 10-week period in my normal state of conditioning to be best prepared for a fight.

I set particular goals for myself during that 10-week process:

#1: Determine his tendencies, strengths and weaknesses by watching tapes of my opponent. Throughout this study, a game plan is developed to put me in the best possible position to win the fight without getting carried away with what my opponent may or may not do. Focus on what you can control—yourself!

#2: Develop the technique to execute your game plan. This doesn't usually include learning new techniques. I am always learning new things, but this is more of a period for refining or sharpening your skills. Drills and repetition are a must.

#3: Mentally prepare for the engagement by visualizing, positive framing and developing a dialog with yourself. See yourself in your mind's eye, believing in your heart that you will win this fight. You must first come to terms with the worst-case scenario, the possibility you may lose. I've often said, "If losing this fight is the worst thing that happens to me in my life, I'm doing well." Keep things in perspective. Enjoy the preparation and the competition.

#4: Achieve peak physical fitness. Nothing in MMA is long and slow, so fashion your training to simulate the fight and your game plan as closely as possible. Perform explosive exercises in round and match-length durations. Sprinting, circuit training and situation sparring are key tools. Make sure you get plenty of rest. It is as important as the work you do.

#5: Tapering is the final step to peak performance. I use a 10-day taper. I am a little older and require more recovery time. Five to seven days might work for a younger fighter. In the taper period, no hard lifting or running. Perform shorter, more specific and controlled sparring sessions with the game plan in mind. Relax, recover and save your energy for the fight.

I was notorious for over-training from my wrestling days into my MMA career. This 10-week peaking phase regiment, along with maintaining a regular training and fitness base out of competition, has made a huge difference in my ability to get the most out of my body and performance.

Good luck!

Bobby gets prepared for an intense season.

WORKOUTS OF DOOM
Part 1

by **Bobby Pittman**

Intensity... we all know what it means and what it can do for us. Whether we're training, sparring, or competing we have to be intense and work hard in order to progress. However, sometimes it's easy to lose our drive and not push ourselves to our limits. For me, if I don't have a competition coming up or some other reason to be in top shape then I end up letting myself off easy. I have to feel challenged to work my hardest. I have to picture my opponent and imagine what he's doing. Is he working harder than me? Is he training more intense than I am? Daydreaming about things like that is what motivates fighters to go out, beat the tar out of each other and put themselves through hell. Because they know that someone else is out there doing it and maybe they are getting tougher. So rather than write a whole page trying to motivate you to go out and train, I'm just going to propose a challenge. Here are four workouts I've tried over the years. Complete them all in four days and you're a true warrior. By the way, puking, bleeding, crying, whining, doubting, falling, and hurting are all allowed. They're almost guaranteed. Just don't give up. There's no limits to what we can do.

Workout 1: This workout requires four people, a track, and a forty-five pound weight plate. Get on a track with each person spaced out evenly (a quarter of a lap in between each person). The first person holds the weight over his head and runs it to the second person. Once the weight is handed off, you must sprint the rest of the lap back around to your starting point, while the second person starts running the weight to the third person, and so on. No putting the weight down and no stopping. You must hurry back to your spot before the weight gets back to you. Each person must complete a total of eight laps.

Workout 2: This workout requires two people. Get with a training partner and just start running. Run at a solid pace (8 minute mile) for 20 minutes. Remember, do not run in a circle. Choose a direction and stick to it so you have the same distance back. Once the twenty minutes is up it's time to turn around. Except now you must carry each other back. Carry your partner until you gas out and then switch. Keep going until you get back to the starting point.

Workout 3: This workout can be done alone. Pick a direction and just start running. Run for about 10-15 minutes at a good pace (8 minute mile). Once the 10-15 minutes is up get down and do as many pushups as you can. Really push yourself for a lot of pushups. Do them on your knees if you have to. Just get a really good burn going. After you can't do anymore, jump up and run back. On the way back keep your arms straight over your head the whole way. When you get back make sure your arms are still attached.

Workout 4: This workout requires a partner and somewhere to spar. I know what you've been thinking. When do we get to spar or fight? If you want it, you got it. Start sparring with your partner. However hard you decide to push each other is just fine. Here's the catch. No time limits, no breaks, no water, nothing. Just spar. It doesn't even matter if you tap or not. The only way to win is to outlast the other guy. Even if it takes all day. My buddy and I once sparred for so long that we couldn't even stand up anymore, but we still didn't stop. We just rolled around until one of us finally gave up. Go for it!

That's it. You've been challenged. There's no excuse why you can't train now. Remember to train smart and safe. This may be something you have to work up to, but these workouts will turn you into a true gladiator. Getting through this will give you the endurance, confidence, and intensity to make it through anything.

WORKOUTS OF DOOM
Part 2

by **Bobby Pittman**

For those of you who completed the workouts from part one of this article, congratulations. If anyone couldn't do it, don't feel bad. This is something you need to work up to – it may even take months depending on your current fitness level. These are workouts I've picked up from world champs, top trainers and elite fighters. I've seen these programs used by NCAA wrestling champions, UFC titleholders, Golden Gloves tournament winners and world class jiu-jitsu fighters. When I talk to them about their workouts I always ask: "What good is all this knowledge if you don't share it with others?" Here are three more of the toughest workouts I've come across.

Dumbbell Challenge
This requires a set of dumbbells (about 20 lbs.)
Grab the dumbbells and just start walking around. Simple? Here's the catch: you can't put the dumbbells down for 20 minutes. No resting them on your legs either. While you're walking, consider that your resting period. The work periods should be done every 30 seconds or so. So go 30 seconds on, 30 seconds off. During the work periods do whatever exercises you think of such as squats, squat jumps, curls, shoulder presses, lateral raises, rows, upright rows, lunges, etc. Be sure to mix it up to get a full body workout. This one is as hard as you make it. After you become used to this you should gradually shorten your rest periods. The ultimate goal is to have no rest periods at all.

Pushing Match
This requires a partner
You and your partner are not actually going to spar; however, you are going to go all out, but there are some rules. First, you must both remain standing. There is no taking each other down. This should look similar to a Greco-Roman wrestling match. However, once you get in position to throw or takedown your opponent just push him away. Pummeling, hand-fighting, and set-ups can be the most exhausting part of a fight, so for this workout just keep things in that phase. You should try to push your opponent around, pummel for inside control, use ducks or drags to take his back, snap him into a

Bobby with K-1 superstar, Michael McDonald

front headlock, work for body locks, inside hand control, and anything else you can think up. This is a great time to work on these skills since you won't have to fear being taken down. Try to keep this workout fast paced and hard and it will pay off in competition.

Jump Rope Challenge
This requires a jump rope and a track
Start running around the track. Complete five laps then do 500 rope jumps. Then run four laps and do 400 rope jumps. Then three laps and 300 rope jumps. Once you've gone from five all the way to one, go back up to five again. The pattern is: 5, 4, 3, 2, 1, 5. This workout will not only make you a cardio machine, but jumping rope will also make you light on your feet which will improve your standup game. Warm your legs up and stretch your calves and Achilles tendons for this one.

If you follow these workouts you will truly benefit from them. I know I did. Workouts are as hard and beneficial as you make them. If you find that you're not pushing yourself hard enough then get a partner to help push you. Find someone who's in better shape than you so you are forced to keep up. This will get you in great shape and make a huge difference in your overall jiu-jitsu, grappling, or no-holds barred game. Take care and good luck!

A Gameplan For Victory

by **Lloyd Irvin, Jr.**

It's never a good idea to enter a match with the intention of "going with the flow." You cannot walk into a fight and expect it to flow in your favor. You have to give some specific thoughts to how you want to play your game and handle your opponent.

My student Mike Fowler was preparing for a match against the Head Instructor of the Yamasaki Academy, Brazilian jiu-jitsu black belt Francisco Neto. Fowler, who has only been training for about three-and-a-half years had a tough task ahead of him.

Some amount of planning is essential. Your moves, your approach to the game, assessing your opponent, the venue and the type of audience are all things you should evaluate. Do you want to be more aggressive than you were at your last match? Do you want to use the new sweep you've been hitting in class? Do you want to get to the venue early to get a good spot in the stands? Do you want to have someone video your opponents' matches? In the absence of a gameplan, all your moves will be a reaction to your opponent's moves. Your entire game will revolve around defense with hardly any proactive action. Do you want to merely react all the time or do you want to play your best moves?

Your chances of winning increase when you plan your moves and use those you're most skilled at. There are four critical factors in winning: a) effective use of technique, b) initiating submissions, c) scoring points, d) successful defense. You have to realize that in order to win you must score points for yourself, initiate submissions, or knock your opponent out. To do this, you need to be proactive and use the right moves. You also have to defend yourself against your opponent and put up a good defense. You must anticipate moves and plan your defense. So going with the flow is actually a lazy way to approach a match.

If you were to see Mike Fowler's gameplan we created for Neto you wouldn't believe how detailed it is. It went from movements, to feet placement, keys for throws, and set-ups for leg submissions – just to name a few.

If you are serious about winning, planning is imperative. Especially at higher-level competition. A gameplan requires sizing up your opponent and developing a strategy to play your best moves and to tackle your opponent's moves. Even if you have never played a par-

ticular opponent before, a certain amount of planning on anticipated moves will give you an advantage.

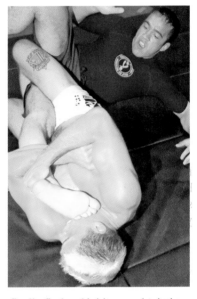

Here's a likely scenario if you don't have a gameplan: a) your opponent may have a good open guard, and you may have problems since you didn't prepare for it, b) your opponent may surprise you, launch an attack and try to dominate the game at a very early stage, c) you may not be able to think up a strategy on the spur of the moment to tackle your opponent until it's too late, d) when you finally find and initiate a submission, time may be up. Here are some of the key issues of mental preparation that I'll cover over the next few issues: a) sizing up your opponent, b) developing a strategy, c) techniques in mental skills training, d) confidence building techniques, e) achieving focus.

Sizing up your opponent is one of the first things you should do in mental preparation: a) analyze the opponent's historical performance in terms of wins and losses and skills or weaknesses displayed, b) recall any tactics that your opponent uses and build a strategy to neutralize them.

We were sure that Neto would be confident against Fowler, because Mike had lost a match to one of his students before and we were sure that Neto could smash his student in training. But this time Fowler didn't have to cut weight for the event and would be at full strength. Being a master of sombo I personally spent a great deal of time drilling leg flows with Mike, believing that if done correctly Neto wouldn't be used to defending my style of leg movements. We respected Neto as a very dangerous opponent and our gameplan showed it. In the end, with a very sound gameplan, Fowler was able to submit Neto with a knee bar just as we planned. So what is your plan? If you don't have one you need to get one ASAP!

Goal Setting and Competing to ~~Win~~ Succeed

by **Lloyd Irvin, Jr.**

Have you ever been curious as to how some people excel at a seemingly impossible pace in jiu-jitsu and submission grappling? What separates the six-year blue belt from the four-year phenom black belt? Some people say it's "natural talent" or "lax promotion standards", and in certain cases, they're right. In most cases, though, the following phrase pretty well sums up the truth of the matter:

"It's not the time you put in, but what you put into the time that matters."

If you've been around the jiu-jitsu scene for awhile, you most likely have come across this cliché. This is the sort of thing coaches in all sports love to tell their athletes. I mean, who wouldn't? It makes you sound wise while still explaining absolutely nothing. Clichéd or not, this phrase is the golden truth, and here at Team Lloyd Irvin, we live by it. In fact, our training systems (The Grappling Blueprint and The Grappling Game Plan) are founded upon it.

But what does it MEAN, and how can I maximize my time? In this month's segment of The Grappling Blueprint breakdown, you're going to find out. I'll even let you in on a not-so-secret that is still inexplicably overlooked by the grappling community: **The key to effective training and rapid improvement lies in the mental approach and the goal-setting process.**

If you've followed our team over the past few years, you already know names like Mike Fowler (four-year BJJ black belt), Brandon Vera (UFC heavyweight contender), Rhadi Ferguson (USA Judo Olympian and ADCC veteran) and Mike Easton (undefeated MMA fighter and BJJ Pan-American silver medalist).

Their goals are well-documented. **Rhadi Ferguson:** accomplished his goal of representing the United States on the biggest stage judo has to offer. **Mike Fowler:** become BJJ black belt world champion. **Brandon Vera:** win and hold both the heavyweight and light-heavyweight UFC belts at the same time. **Mike Easton:** become the number-one 145-pound MMA fighter in the world and win a BJJ world title. The latter three are all well on their way to accomplishing their stated goals.

Before you begin competition (or anything in life for that matter), it is imperative to identify what you hope to achieve and what benefit you hope to derive from your efforts. Here's another nugget of wisdom that probably deserves its own motivational poster: **"If a man does not know which harbor he is seeking, no light will be enough to guide him."**

What do you want out of your training? What, if you could choose, would be the ultimate culmination of your hours spent in the gym, all the sleep lost in tape study or money spent going from event to event in the quest for grappling glory? First place in a blue belt division? A pat on the back from your instructor? Holding two UFC title belts at the same time? How will you reach the goals you have set for yourself? Are you in the place and surrounded by the people you will need to take your best shot at success?

While you ponder those answers, let me tell you about two of my students. The first is further along the path towards his goals than the second, but both have striking similarities that one climbing the ladder of upper-tier competition may be interested in. Mike Fowler is the original product of our training systems, The Grappling Blueprint (www.thegrapplingblueprint.com) and The Grappling Gameplan (www.thegrapplinggameplan.com). A few years ago, I put him on the world stage and made my intentions clear: I would take Mike from an unknown with no appreciable grappling background and turn him into one of America's brightest homegrown jiu-jitsu stars. People doubted us, but we did it. It's pretty hard to argue with three international medals and a second place finish at the 2006 North American Abu Dhabi Trials in only five years of total training!

The next is Ryan Hall, who with only two and half years of training, already has 139 triangle submissions in competition as of my writing today.

Good Training,
Lloyd Irvin, Jr.

Fight Preparation

by **Bas Rutten**

THE NIGHT BEFORE THE FIGHT

If you find it difficult to sleep, just think about the fight. Other people will say you have to think about something else, but you know as well as I do, that's impossible. I found it relaxing to visualize the fight in my mind, "seeing yourself fight, countering his moves, testing him out, etc." This always made me fall asleep very fast. Even if you can't sleep and just lay there, your body is resting. Don't start reading things, just let your mind wander off and relax.

I speak from experience, why? Going from Holland to Japan means "day time" for you is at night—6:00AM in Japan is 11:00PM in Holland. You can't sleep at night so just stay awake and relax. Whatever you do, DO NOT sleep during the day if you fight outside the country and you are tired. I know it's difficult, but if you do it, you can't fall asleep anymore at night! If you come from America to Japan (you have a different jet lag), you fall asleep early and wake up early so you have at least your eight hours.

Make sure you absolutely don't use sleeping pills; they WILL slow you down, no matter what other people say. Melatonin is something you can use because it's natural, but the best thing: *don't use anything!*

THE DAY OF THE FIGHT

About food again: DO NOT eat something on the day of the fight that you have never tried before. I don't care if your friends tell you it's the best. Never EVER do a thing like that, so no carb shakes, energy drinks or anything you've never tried before. Remember, everything you eat has a different outcome when you mix it with the adrenaline your body produces before the fight!

I ate whole wheat bread with marmalade jelly (for some reason that stops my muscles from building up lactic acid, try it!) and drank water, nothing else. Stay away from dairy products: cheese, milk, etc. Stop eating at least three hours before the fight. Digesting takes away a lot of energy, which you will need in the fight.

Keep your "aggressive" friends away from you, the ones who tell you all the freaking time, "Rip his head off!" and "Beat the crap out of him!" You don't need these comments and they won't do you any good. Ask any of my friends if I had people who said ONE thing like that to me. They'll tell you I threw them out of my locker room; you don't need that, your mind needs to be relaxed.

Think about this: Why do you think you are better mentally when training? When you are in the gym, you are relaxed and don't have all those variables associated with the fight itself. Training and fighting are two totally different things. That's why I hate those "dumb guys" who never fought and tell me all the time, "Yeah, I tapped his ass so many times when I was sparring with him (and they are talking about a champion)." Please, if you are that good, why don't you fight yourself? Try to slap on that same arm bar when your friends, family members and the whole world watch you fight. Yep, that's right, that's why you don't fight and the other ones DO. They take the chance you aren't willing to take. What you also don't need is TWO or even THREE people telling you what to do, and they all tell you something different—that's even worse.

Guys, you trained now for a long time, you KNOW what to do, you need only ONE coach who tells you like three to five major things that you need to work on—not 50, because it will make your head spin!

Also, stay away from the "what ifs", because once you start thinking like that, you mess up your mind. Example: "What if he counters my right straight?" or "What if I shoot in and he knees me in the head?" Once you start thinking like that, you are gone. You are going to be afraid to throw a punch or kick or go for a takedown.

Make sure you warm up hard—that's my motto. I always did ten rounds of only ONE minute Thai Pad training, but 100% not 99%. Do sprawls, abs, "pump up" every muscle you can think of so your body gets used to that. Remember, you also get tired because your muscles build themselves up with lactic acid. If you don't warm up hard, your abs or upper body will build up with lactic acid during the fight. Now the muscles around your lungs (chest, abs, back, shoulders) will keep your lungs from "breathing freely" anymore. That's why I warmed up hard in the dressing room and still do in training. Your body will learn how to deal with that right away. Trust me, you DO NOT want to find that out during the fight. THIS, my friends, together with the adrenaline, is why you think when you're fighting: "Why do I get tired so fast? I never get tired so fast in training!"

As I said before, make sure you are totally relaxed too because stress pumps up those muscles too AND let's not forget your brain. It needs to think freely too so being relaxed is the key to victory. Take a look at fighters like Sakuraba and Fedor. When they fight, they are totally relaxed! This will give them WAY more energy than the fighters who are fighting with a lot of stress.

I always enjoyed listening to relaxing music on my mini-disc player, and together with my Game Boy, I was somewhere else and not in the fight. Plus I am a master in Tetris now!

Every fighter has thoughts running through his mind so you must learn to deal with it and always RELAX!

THE FIGHT!

by **Bas Rutten**

Before I go further, I want to remind you about something very important: Always bring your fight gear with you when flying to an event. Bring it as a "carry on" item, and don't take the risk of the airline losing your bags so you don't have your own gear for the fight. This is one mental variable that should never be in question.

OK, you are warmed up and ready to enter the ring.

THE STARE DOWN
Personally I think it's a bunch of BS—you don't need it—why do you need to look at somebody angry? It didn't scare me or anything. Just fight! That's what you came for, right?

If your opponent talks shit, he's probably insecure so take that as a positive for you. A "stare down" might be cool for the audience, but it puts more pressure on you. Just look at the ground. I personally always looked at my opponent's belly. If I saw it trembling from nerves, I knew I had the mental edge. Try it out; it works like a charm.

If you are comfortable with the "stare down", be my guest because promotions need colorful people. And that's another thing, tattoos aren't intimidating so don't sweat them.

THE GAME PLAN
Try to stick to your game plan knowing your opponent tries to take you out of it. A lot of fighters go into the fight with a game plan, get hit with a good shot and then retreat to an old routine.

He hit you, so what? It could be a lucky shot so stick with your game plan and try it again. It's always good to have a back-up plan as well.

A lot of fighters get hit and it sticks with them: "He hit me! He shouldn't have hit me!" BAM! You get another shot upside your head because your mind wasn't focusing; you were too busy getting tagged again. Let it go.

Unnecessary ring bravado is another thing I don't understand. When your opponent hits YOU, you laugh as if you want to show him it doesn't hurt. Don't laugh because he just scored a point (and in 90% of the cases, you DID get hurt and are bluffing anyway). Are you trying to intimidate him?

If you want to laugh when you get hit, go ahead, but fire back with everything you got, shoot him another smile and ask him to hit you

again. See? NOW you're in his mind and that's where you want to be.

If you're nervous, start the fight by moving backwards (not straight backwards, always circle) and get used to the ring. Let him make the first move and get used to his reach. Throw a hard jab and see how he reacts. Does he bring his hands up real fast? Hit him again with a left to the head, and then add a straight right to the body. If that works, repeat the action, but now add a left hook to his head. See how effective this is? Because the straight right to his body after the left to the head worked, now he thinks he'll be "prepared" for that straight right. Throw the straight right again, he'll block it and THAT will open himself up for the left hook you're now going to add. Works like a charm.

A FEW OTHER TRICKS
When the fight starts, and you have a good kick, kick him with everything you have. But the kick has to be SO hard that he feels the impact and thinks, "I better block that kick because if I don't, I am going to get hurt." BAM! You are inside his head again. You can also try this with the straight right hand. The objective is to break him down. If he's known for a special move, train to counter it.

These are all ways to get inside his head, and like I've said many times before, fighting is 90% mental.

Check out something new I've just added to my site at www.drill-forskill.com. Also check out the Big DVDs of Combat. Do you want to become a teacher under me? Go to the website, www.bas-rutten.tv, and click on "MMA System". This one is going to take time and a lot of work, but I assure you, there is no other program like this, and you will become a phenomenal teacher. That's my promise to you!

Till next time!

Bas "El Guapo" Rutten

Judo: Don't Call it a Comback! It Never Left!

by **Mike Swain**

With MMA constantly evolving, takedowns are on the rise as a popular topic. These days, there's a lot more to takedowns than just doubles and singles. Judo is actually being thrown into the mix of vocabulary when discussing MMA. They say it is on its way back; I say it never left.

Many people ask me what happened to judo in the US and do I think it will ever come back to its glory days in the 1960s, when magazine covers and articles were about judo? My answer is simple. "Try it! You will like it." You will like it because it's a great cardiovascular workout, a standing and ground workout and because it is one of the only ways you can go all-out practicing takedowns without getting too busted up. If you are not an MMA fighter, you will like it because you can learn at your own pace. It teaches the fundamentals of all martial arts: respect and discipline for the mind, body and spirit.

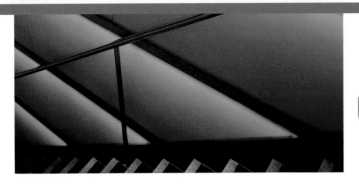

As a four-time Olympian, I have traveled all over the world competing and training for half my life in judo. Believe me, it is the best-kept secret on the fight scene today. Unfortunately the best US training hubs are few and far between, spread out all over: San Jose, CA, New York metropolitan area, and Miami, FL are some of the hot beds. However, step outside the US into Japan, France, Germany, Brazil and Korea, and you will see why judo training is second to none in takedowns. You will see the hardcore training of throws, which hone your skills of balance, speed and timing. You also may be surprised to see an awesome ground game (chokes, arm-locks and pins), which has been there long before Brazilian jiu-jitsu ever started.

Transitioning is probably the most important aspect of judo that relates to MMA. Transitioning is the point between taking someone down and securing a submission, choke or pin (holding someone for 25 seconds is the same as submitting in judo). Let's face it, if you can't get out in 25 seconds, nothing good can happen to you after that. Ha! There is a split second or two when your opponent's mind loses concentration after a takedown or throw. During that split second is when you must train your body to move in for the submission or at least a controlling position. Judo practice is one of the best ways to train the transition because you have four ways to win: standing (throws) and ground (chokes, arm-locks and pins). Your strategy is to throw first and get your opponent to the ground, and then if needed, finish on the ground. You must constantly be attacking from standing, ground and in-between.

Yes, judo probably missed the commercial dollars of schools in every strip mall because of poor marketing, and they are still waiting for the Judo Kid movie to educate the layman. On the flip side, judo has been an Olympic sport since 1964. Each Olympics, we witness new variations of throws or ground techniques due to the ever-evolving Olympic athletes and their quest for the Gold. In the end, judo is still judo with the same core set of throws, holds, chokes and arm-locks, practiced in over 180 countries worldwide. It's always been here and always will. All you have to do is try it.

LOSING TO WIN

by **Mike Swain**

Let's face it! Everyone loses at some point in their career. MMA, judo, boxing and wrestling are all individual sports pitting you against one individual. Championships are set up to crown only one winner with many losers. Learning from your losses is essential to winning.

Dealing with loss tells you and others who you really are. When faced with a loss, I tell my fighters to look in the mirror and tell yourself why you lost. Perhaps it was a mental mistake, not enough endurance or lack of technique. Whatever the reason, and there is a reason for every loss, don't blame it on others no matter what bad call occurred, how strong your opponent was, or what problem you thought you had with your coach.

Understand within yourself that you have accountability for the loss, and that losing is part of the process on the path to winning. Champions can tell you precisely why they lost, and what they will do to fix it. They know that every loss makes them learn what it takes to win.

Speaking from my own experience, when I won a silver medal at the 1985 World Championships in Seoul, Korea, I became the first American to ever fight in the Finals of a world championship since it's inception in 1956. In front of thousands of screaming spectators, I lost a decision to the defending Olympic champion from Korea in Korea. When I walked off the mat, people congratulated me on a well-fought match, but all I could think about was what I have to do to win the gold next time. I thought I had given everything I had, but understood within myself that I had not. I remember the exact moment during the match where I was too aggressive and off balance.

That silver medal, or first place loser as some referred to it, was a bitter sweet feeling. But if it weren't for that loss, I am not sure I would have won the Worlds two years later in Germany. A personal friend of mine, Isao Okano, the 1964 Olympic champion and perhaps the greatest judo fighter ever, summed it up best in his book, Vital Judo: "I know that some men attempt to sidestep the issue of responsibility involved in winning and losing by saying that is a matter of luck. But anyone who entertains this attitude is already disqualified for consideration as a true judo winner. A person who lacks the willpower to look extreme difficulties in the face has no luck. Luck does not wait for one: One must make one's luck."

Martin Rooney, elite trainer and director at the Parisi Speed School of Fitness, one of the most sought after places for physical conditioning in the country (www.parisischool.com), said in his book, Train to Win: "As humans we either do things to feel great or to avoid feeling bad. Understanding this important concept will help the athlete to deal better with loss. Do not rationalize the result to avoid feeling bad, but realize that what we aspire is to have our dreams come true athletically, so that we feel great. When we really see this, then we will see losing as a chance to get closer to feeling great and improvement as an athlete and a person."

HOW TO TELL A WINNER FROM A LOSER

- A winner says "Let's find out." A loser says, "Nobody knows."
- When a winner makes a mistake, he says, "I was wrong." When a loser makes a mistake, he says, "It wasn't my fault."
- A winner goes through a problem. A loser goes around it and never gets past it.
- A winner makes commitments. A loser makes promises.
- A winner says, "I'm good, but not as good as I ought to be." A loser says, "I'm not as bad as a lot of other people."
- A winner tries to learn from those who are superior to him. A loser tries to tear down those who are superior to him.
- A winner says, "There ought to be a better way to do it." A loser says, "That is the way it has always been done."

Read these over and try and see when you were guilty of being a loser. If you find any and correct them for the future, growth and improvement are sure to follow.

CSW Game Assessment

by **Erik Paulson**

1. **Honesty** plays a major role in the total development of your grappling game.

2. You must be your own best and worst **critic** when assessing the whole picture.

3. Remember, grappling is a **puzzle**, a chess game that comes together.

4. To see where your level fits into the puzzle, you MUST attend training sessions, classes and competitions or fights that make you **contest** your skill.

5. The level of your opponents should at least **challenge your skills** and abilities, so it is important to drill with lesser, equal and greater opponents who allow you to try different games or will improve your current game.

6. Practice or training is about finding yourself, a **self-discovery**. It's known as "chopping blocks". This is where your are developing and honing your basics, learning your basics, and learning new skills and techniques to add to your game.

7. On the mat in training or in practice, there is no **winning** or **losing**…just training.

8. In competition, it is an accomplishment when you win. It is **self-discovery** when you lose.

9. The "Did you make him tap?" mentality is all **ego**-based and **small mindedness** gets old quick. Who cares! The key rests on you being on the mat, training hard and smart and keeping your mouth shut. Put emphasis on concentrating on your own movement and stamina, as well as skill, speed, strength and methodology.

10. **Tapping speaks for itself**; when you're training and you get caught and tap out, you learn. If training wasn't about learning, you would have to say it isn't productive.

11. If you are doing all the tapping, you have a lot of growth ahead of you. Be **grateful** when you are tapped out.

12. Quite possible, if not being tapped out, it is time to find people who will make you tap again if **self-improvement** is one of your goals.

13. If you are at the top of your club, then **help others** improve. In turn, this will help you to improve. You can grow by teaching others how to catch you or attack your weaknesses.

14. In wrestling practice, nobody asks, "Did you take him down?" or "Did you stick him or pin him?" Of course **both**, you're supposed to. **It's practice!!!**

15. After boxing, sparring or training sessions, people don't ask, "Did you get jabbed, crossed or hooked?" or "Did you knock him out or get knocked out?" Of course, it's **training**. It's **preparation** for when it does matter…your fight or match or tournament.

16. **Mannerisms** are just as important. Shake hands after the fight, win, lose or draw.

17. Keep a clear mind by focusing on what is true and positive. Do not speculate about anything. Think about how you will **improve** your next training session and walk out of your gym knowing that tomorrow will be better.

18. **Smile**. Remember, you chose this sport because you decided you liked it, so **enjoy it** and reap the fruits of your dedicated training.

19. Remember, we are **all** important and **everyone** matters.

20. **Consistency** is king!

THE WALL SURVIVAL DRILL

by **Erik Paulson**

In boxing this drill is also referred to as a *corner drill*, used as an essential element of a fighter's ability to take and defend against a punch, and to see where the attack is coming from. It dates back to the Filipino boxing era and was employed by many knife fighters to teach them how to acknowledge the lines of attack and the body movement necessary to set up the combinations following the primary attack. Dan Inosanto originally trained many of his students and fighters with this drill that was passed down through several of his teachers and trainers.

This drill was originally shown to me by Tim Tackett and Burt Poe, who once trained a specific few in their garage and was kind enough to share some great information every Wednesday night in Redlands, California.

The drill originally consisted of one person standing against the wall with both hands up while the other would punch non-stop to the head and body for one or three minutes. This drill conditions the person getting hit as to how to take a shot and cover. For the feeder, it tests his/her arm endurance to punch from one-three minutes straight, working on angles and attacks.

This drill is great for developing your pain threshold. Everybody loves to dish out pain, however very few can accept or put up with it. For a fighter, it comes with the territory.

During my fight career, this drill was the "bread and butter" for my daily training routine. I give credit to this drill for saving my face and brain to take as little abuse as possible, while remaining in the slugging range both standing and on the ground. This drill became a substantial part of my daily rounds of stand-up training. I used it as my "resting" rounds between my punching, kneeing, kicking and sprawling.

Instead of stopping and resting, I was thrown into the corner on the ropes and had my trainer throw all types of angles and ranges of punches at me. Using only two guards, the *windshield wiper defense* and the *double pillar defense*, along with head and shoulder movement, I was able to read my opponent's intentions and attack combinations. My whole theory was to remain fighting toe to toe and not get hit. If I didn't use this standing, I used it on the ground when I was getting my head punched at. I modified this drill to best fit my body structure and style of fighting.

I changed it into five parts:

1. A) Windshield wiper defense: I've found to be the best punch cover defense against a boxer (rear hand catches everything).

B) Double Pillar Defense: Great for punch, kick and elbow defense, best used against a kickboxer (both hands, forearms and elbows block everything).

2. Clinching on the 1/2 beat. You should clinch on either the 1/2, 1 1/2, 2 1/2 or 3 1/2 beat motion. No more than 4 punches should be thrown at you before clinching. Clinching should be done on 3 levels: 1. Head 2. Body 3. Legs (drill teaches timing on when to engage).

3. Striker stopping, stuffing or nullifying the clinch attempt. This trains the striker how to stop the grappler from completing or playing his game (keeps you standing).

4. Shooting or clinching, getting stopped, then re-shooting or clinching makes you aggressive and persistent at a non-stop pace.

5. Puncher stops clinch or shoot and re-shoots. This trains the striker how to stop the clinch or shot attempt and re-shoot to go on top.

This drill is specifically formulated for the MMA fighter. It teaches you a defense no one can penetrate, timing the shot, stopping the shot and re-shooting to put your opponent on his back so you can control top side. It's great for stand-up, on the ground and succeeding without getting hit.

This drill is also easy to find training partners for. All you need to do is walk into your gym and yell, "Who wants to punch me in the head!" I guarantee you'll get a few takers.

Remember to start slow and then pick up the pace. Mix 1 1/2 punch combos, break in and out and step in at three different angles: 1. Diagonal left 2. Straight in 3. Diagonal right.

Start out with conventional boxing's five punches: jab, cross, uppercut, hook and overhand. Then add backfist, hammerfist, spinning backfist, liver shot, spleen shot, kidney shot and heart punch.

Mix and match punches, change the rhythm of attack speed, and fake or feint your way in!

HAVE FUN, GET GOOD AND LEARN HOW NOT TO GET HIT!

Joints, Tendons and Ligaments on STEROIDS!

by **Jacob Geissler, Sports Nutrition B.A.**

I hope I choked your attention with this headline. It would be foolish to recommend steroids for joint, tendon and ligament health because steroids do the exact opposite. Yes, they build muscle strength, but not tendon strength. If you fall victim to joint, tendon or ligament (for brevity sake, "joints" will stand for joint, ligament and tendon) issues and steroids are pushed onto you, just send them back with an educated grin.

Is all hope lost once our joints start to break down due to over-training and age? No, there is a very successful protocol I implement with all my clients (fighters and regular folks who train). The protocol below can be used when injured, but it can be used as a PREVENTATIVE to not getting injured and building joint strength.

Step 1:
You must eliminate all sugar, refined flours (white pasta, white bread, cheap cereals, etc.) and fried foods. A bad diet is the curse of all illness. The above foods cause a rise in insulin which is an inflammatory hormone.

Step 2:
Drink AT LEAST one gallon of water a day to flush toxins and hydrate the body.

Step 3:
Cissus Quandrangularis is a herb from India that was used to speed fracture healing by 50%! A new innovative supplement company called USPLabs (www.usplabsdirect.com) has filed a patent and discovered that Cissus promotes nutrient flow to the injured joints to speed recovery from sprains, breaks and tendonitis. Cissus also promotes joint strength that is valuable to any athlete.

Step 4:
Proteolytic enzymes are enzymes used by the body for protein digestion. A recent discovery in the scientific community says that proteolytic enzymes attack inflammation. Labrada Nutrition makes a product specifically designed for this purpose, but you can find proteolytic enzymes in any supplement store.

Step 5:
One tablespoon of olive oil will act as an absorbing agent (carrier) for the above supplements. Olive oil contains too many medicinal benefits to name for the scope of this article, but of importance, olive oil is also an anti-inflammatory.

Step 6:
Essential Fatty Acids (EFAs) and fish oil also have multiple health benefits. Fish oil is an anti-inflammatory. I would guess that 80% of the world is deficient in EFAs. EFAs should be consumed regardless of injury and for general health.

Step 7:
REST! REST! REST! Injuries will only get worse if you keep training with the same intensity. Make sure you add active recovery training (rehabilitation approach to training).

Step 8:
How do we implement the plan? Simple!

45 minutes before training:
1 cap of Cissus
1 cap of proteolytic enzymes
1 tablespoon olive oil

Before bed:
1 cap of Cissus
1 cap of proteolytic enzymes
1 tablespoon olive oil

You should take 3 caps of EFAs three times a day with meals.

The above protocol has worked miracles for many of my clients. Remember that injuries happen due to over use, bad posture or bad exercise form. Please do not expect an overnight miracle, but you should see results in 3-6 weeks.

A serious note: If you are injured, please take 3-6 weeks with a rehabilitation approach to training.

Second serious note: The above protocol will strengthen your joints to new heights so implement it before you get injured!

Training for MMA

by **Jason "Mayhem" Miller**

Increasingly, Mayhem Monkeys ask me how to train and prepare for fights in their parts of America…this is how I train. I've made the mistakes so you don't have to.

GEAR UP

First off, before you step foot in the training room, make sure you have the correct gear. I'm not saying you have to spend a truckload of cash, but come with the proper gear so you don't hurt yourself and training partners. This means if you're throwing knees, get knee pads, throwing kicks and shinpads, and if you like to block punches with your face, wear headgear. Don't fall into the tough guy category and go headgear-less. I missed one big payday because of a silly cut and never went without it again.

CORRECT PREPARATION

If you are preparing for wrestling, wrestle. If preparing for BJJ, do BJJ. If preparing for pairs ice skating, strap on your leotard and get to work. I'm not saying to neglect your conditioning, but if your intention is to fight mixed martial arts, then you must have time set aside to focus on a total MMA workout that includes all aspects of the game. All too often, people focus on the areas separately and then try to throw them together when its game time. Dumb as a sack of onions. Two days a week = full MMA training.

SHARPEN

Focus on particular areas. Prepare with your opponent in mind. Cater to his weaknesses and your strengths. You have to drill situations that your opponent is good at, and practice avoiding them, until you're sick and damn tired of it. Have days where you work "situational drilling"; it's something we do very often at Team Quest Temecula for MMA and has worked very well for Cobra Kai Jiujitsu in the jiu-jitsu world. At least one day a week, start in a situation (even bad ones) like having their back or someone having your back, and see how much and quickly your game improves.

CONDITION

Make sure to get two tough workouts a week that focus primarily on getting your heart rate kicking like a midget in a headlock. Sprints are an easy way. For example, do four 5- minute rounds on a treadmill. The first one a warm-up, 6mph, then start the TOUGH workout, running at level 12 (or as fast as you/the treadmill can) for one minute, then down to 6 for one minute. Do 12, then 6, then at the end of that "round", you can walk at 3.5mph, then back to the sprint workout. A conditioning circuit can also be worked in. Weights at high reps prepare your body and keep the muscles strong. A workout I call the "Hendo" is basically 14 machine motions at 100 repetitions. Alternate push and pull, upper and lower body, and attempt to get through it in 25 minutes, sissy!

DIET

Your diet could be a whole other article, depending on whether you are trying to lose weight or gain weight, but a good rule of thumb is plenty of green vegetables and whole grains throughout the day. Many athletes have the tendency to overkill it with protein, only to store it as fat. That protein overload tends to make me feel sluggish, not a great feeling when someone is throwing his fists at your facial tissue. If you have trouble eating a lot of green vegetables throughout the day, try a supplement like Light Force Greens, that although if you aren't used to it, tastes a bit like grass clippings, supplies you with all the greens you need to feel great for the day.

REST

Make sure to take adequate rest time. Along with diet, this is a very important part of your training regimen, even though it seems like you aren't even training. When you're resting and recovering, you can watch tapes and study up on moves, but make sure to give yourself time away from the beautiful art of MMA, or instead of a gorgeous girlfriend, she becomes a nagging wife.

10 Tips for Success in BJJ Competition

by **Marcio Feitosa**

1. Be prepared. Train hard because when the pressure is on and the fight is close, the only thing keeping you going is the fact you trained hard for that moment. Extraordinary dedication equals extraordinary results. Multiple-time champion Fredson Paixao is one of my training partners, and I have a lot of respect for him. While the rest of Rio is going to bed, you can find him every morning at Copacabana Beach at 6 AM, running sprints on the beach, doing push-ups and pull-ups. After that, he begins his Brazilian jiu-jitsu (BJJ) training!

2. Use strategy. You must be a strategist to be a good competitor. First you have to know what kind of fighter you are and understand your game—weaknesses and strengths. Also know where your opponent will want to take the fight and do the opposite. One of the biggest surprises in the 2005 ADCC Submission Wrestling Championships was in the open weight class division semifinals between Marcelo Garcia and Ronaldo "Jacare" Souza. Normally known for having great takedowns, Jacare surprised everyone by pulling closed guard and catching Marcelo Garcia in a Kimura. By doing something unexpected, Jacare turned a potentially difficult fight into a quick and easy win.

3. Remember, BJJ isn't math – it's Calculus. Try to learn all facets of BJJ, and though it's not an exact science—you always have to be ready to improvise during competition— expect the unexpected. At the 2005 Pan American Championships, during the Black Belt Middleweight semifinals, Felipe "Cranivata" Simao passed Andre Galvao's guard and took his back, securing what appeared to be a very tight choke. Clearly this was not what Galvao was expecting, but he maintained his composure and worked first to get back to Cranivata's guard. Galvao then passed, mounted and submitted Cranivata, overcoming what appeared to be an insurmountable obstacle. Even if things didn't go exactly as planned, Galvao never believed he was out of the fight.

4. Be confident. The goal of competition is not to earn medals. It's an opportunity to test one's limits. Your opponent is not your enemy; he is actually someone helping you to see what you have inside and to test yourself.

5. Shut out distractions. Focus on things you can control and forget about when you think the referee made a bad call, or how good your opponent is, or the pressure from the crowd. I lost so many fights because I always fought two opponents: my opponent and the referee! By the time I was yelling at the referee, my opponent was already kicking my ass. Now I realize I can only control my own state of mind.

6. Train hard, but train smart. If you are injured, you cannot train consistently. Respect your limits, and don't be too proud to tap during training.

7. Compete consistently. Experience is an important part of any competition, and the more you compete, the more experience you gain. Just training at the school will not get you ready enough. The more practice in dealing with what transpires in competition, the better you will become.

8. Learn from your mistakes. BJJ is like chess for your body. The ones who think are the ones who will succeed, not the ones who just train hard. If you make a mistake, reflect on it, dissect it and learn how to avoid that situation again.

9. Study the game. Use the top athletes in the game as a manual for your references. Try to emulate someone else's game. Watch top athletes, who have similar physical qualities, compete and try to use their positions and strategies.

10. Study the rules. Most of the time, six or seven minutes is not long enough to win just with talent alone. All of the top competitors are able to use strategy to their advantage. Not enough competitors know all of the nuances of the rules, and often, it costs them the fight. Everyone should check out www.cbjj.com.br/english to familiarize themselves with the rules of the game.

Don't Get Mad.
Get M.A.D.D.R.!

by **Marcio Feitosa**

Let's talk about one of the biggest challenges for anyone who studies Brazilian jiu-jitsu (BJJ): the ability to apply newly-learned submissions when a training partner applies resistance. One can learn to execute a technique perfectly with a compliant partner, but the ability to successfully perform a submission with resistance is a moment of joy on the mats, and can be a testament to one's mastery of a particular technique.

While it is completely possible for one to become a great competitor without mastering submissions, it will not allow you to develop a technical game. Learning to build a strategy to win matches based upon scoring points and advantages is very important, but only emphasizing a points-based strategy is one reason why some tournament winners are not always the competitors with the best technique. One cannot, however, truly master BJJ without mastering submissions. The essence of BJJ lies in learning how to apply both control and submission holds–don't rob yourself the beauty of our art!

When you think about mastering submissions, think about getting **MADDR:**

Mental
Approach;
Drilling Techniques;
Drilling Positions;
Reflect

MENTAL APPROACH: This is perhaps the most important element of training any aspect of BJJ, but is particularly important here. Your mental approach to training will truly dictate how much progress you make. Your day-to-day training should not be focused on scoring points or advantages only. Remember:

If you reach a position where you are in control, don't just stop there. *Your biggest goal is reaching the submission*. Allow yourself to take risks during training, and don't be afraid to give up position. Eventually, you will learn to correct mistakes and discover the details that are impossible to obtain simply through drilling techniques.

When you are in a bad position, *don't fear the submission*. Keep moving and trying to escape. Observing how your partners move in trying to submit you will not only help you to master your escapes, but will also give you a much better understanding about how to attack.

DRILL TECHNIQUES: Of course, our objective is to be able to apply the technique on a resisting partner. But, we can't forget that mastery of the mechanics of the submission is a vital step in that process. We need to learn the details of the position so we can add the speed and momentum necessary to make the submission work. Remember, if we have the ability to execute a technique smoothly, we have the ability to apply it slowly, quickly, gently, or with power.

DRILL POSITIONS: When sparring we spend most of our time passing and defending the guard. Sharpening submissions from side mount, knee to belly, mount and back mount requires a different type of training tool. In order to get better at submissions from all positions, it is very important to set time aside for specific positional drills. For instance, we start from a set position such as the mount. One partner will try to apply submissions and the other partner's goal is to either defend or escape if possible. Personally, I like to execute this type of training at least two times a week, with three minutes for each partner in each position (mount, back mount, side control).

REFLECT: Finally, your training isn't over just because you've left the mats. After a training session, spend some time to think about what happened during class. Taking notes on your training and the positions you've learned is a good way to reflect. The person who gets the best results from training isn't always the one who spends the most time on the mats–it's the one who is able to have the most *quality* time on the mats. BJJ is just as much a mental exercise as a physical one, so don't neglect exercising the most important muscle of all: your brain!

THE RUBBER GUARD MYTH

by **Eddie Bravo**

Many believe the rubber guard is just a myth or over-hyped marketing tool that would be ineffective in MMA. I mean, how would I know what guard works best for MMA when I've never fought before?

Music has been my passion since age 14, but I got into martial arts to keep in shape. It was a hobby that ran amok. I wanted my BJJ to be as MMA ready as possible, just in case the music business didn't work out and I needed to make some cash.

For the past ten years, I've been working on no-gi submission set-ups. Even though my music career began to take flight, I believe I've designed an effective guard style for MMA. About 80% of MMA fighters today use what I call "double wrist control guard" when trying to set up a submission from the guard. Start paying attention when watching fights and you'll see that most fighters go right to this style of guard.

They control both of their opponent's wrists with their hands and usually keep their feet on their opponent's hips or around their waists, throwing up triangle attempts with little control of their opponent's upper body. The "double wrist control guard" isn't about keeping your opponent's posture broken and isn't designed to keep him locked between your legs either.

Controlling someone's wrists only works for seconds at a time before your opponent will break free. This allows your opponent to posture up, throwing punches and backing out of your guard whenever he wishes. Playing "double wrist control guard" also makes it easy for your opponent to posture out of triangles, because you have zero control of his upper body.

The "double wrist control guard" works sometimes, but in a sport where you may only get one chance, "sometimes" isn't good enough. Rodrigo Nogueira is one the greatest fighters who ever lived and he's a true MMA legend. He's also a master of the "double wrist control guard", but he hasn't hit a triangle using

this guard in over four years. Why? Because he chooses not to control his opponent's posture when setting up submissions off his back.

When playing the rubber guard, your opponent's posture must be completely broken down at all times. If not, then you are not playing the rubber guard. Once your opponent's posture is broken down, you must keep it down, always squeezing your opponent with your legs. This is crucial for preventing the guard pass. Once under complete control, you can immediately go to *mission control* or *new york* or *the pump* or the *invisible collar*. All of these positions are in the clinch, making it very difficult for your opponent to punch you with any power. These clinch positions also make it harder for your opponent to pull out of submissions compared to when using the "double wrist control guard".

At my academy, the rubber guard is not a myth. It is a very offensive guard with an ironically built-in high level defense as well. BUT it takes a real commitment to master. After three years of teaching my 10th Planet Jiu Jitsu style, only about five of my students can effectively play the rubber guard consistently. You must really put in serious hours and years on the mat drilling *mission control* or *the zombie, etc*. to make the rubber guard effective.

Shigeki Matsuda, a Japanese pro boxer and brown belt in my system, is currently my top student in the rubber guard department. Shigeki is finally at that stage where he goes to the rubber guard not to try and work it into his game; it is his game. He will be making his MMA debut right about the time my new book, *10th Planet Jiu Jitsu: Mastering The Rubber Guard*, hits the shelves. Hopefully by then, more fighters will open their minds to a different way of playing guard in MMA. I really do believe it could help minimize stalemates in the guard. If I'm right, that could translate to fewer boring fights in the future.

Pulling Guard

by **Eddie Bravo**

I've taken a lot of heat for pulling guard on MMA forums over the years, especially The Underground Forum at mma.tv. Apparently it's not the manly thing to do in a fight since pulling guard means you're immediately falling to your back, trying to keep your opponent between your legs.

I guess it's really hard for some people to watch two grown men grapple and not think of it as a sexual act as well. If you've never seen anyone do BJJ before, it would be normal to think of the guard in a sexual way, but when you're struggling on the mat with some dude who's trying to hyper-extend your arm or squeeze the life out of your neck; sex is the last thing on your mind. All you know is if you're on your back and you DON'T keep your opponent between your legs, you're in serious danger of being tapped out—and no one likes the feeling of that—NO ONE!

Even though I've pulled guard in every single match in my BJJ career, I would almost always choose the top position over the guard IF my opponent gave me the choice. The reason I've always pulled guard from the start of my BJJ career stems from tournaments costing around $60 to enter and most blue belt matches were only about six minutes long.

That is very little time to really play and set up different strategies. Trust me, when the pressure is on, six minutes goes by in a flash. Six weeks of hard training, dieting and cutting weight all boils down to six minutes. So if you try to set up takedowns, while countering your opponent's own takedown attempts, that could be two, three, even four minutes of your precious BJJ time spent dancing around, trying to prove the supremacy of the best wrestler.

And that leaves what, maybe three minutes to finish your opponent on the ground? All that suffering for $60 and only three minutes of actual Brazilian jiu-jitsu! F that! How about I pull guard and we get the party started?

I wanted ALL those six minutes to take place in the BJJ world, not the judo or wrestling world. That's why I pulled guard in every one of my matches—to get my money's worth—NOT because I thought it was the best strategy in a fight. Plus I was usually on my back anyway at Jean Jacques Machado's school, so I was very comfortable there. My feeble little body kept me from playing too much top game during the early years.

Photo: Kris Shaw   www.wcgalleries.com

Is pulling guard a stupid thing to do in MMA? Most people think so. Why? I'm not sure, but it might be because we haven't seen too many MMA fighters win at a high rate with that strategy, or it might be a little of that, mixed in with the whole "missionary" thing. But I think all of that is about to change. Will pulling guard ever be thought of as a great strategy or dangerous weapon in MMA? Well, if the rubber guard is mastered, it definitely can be.

Talk to Pride fighter Shinya Aoki or UFC fighter Dean Lister about that. Both men have learned the rubber guard and have "pulled guard" in big shows and won. Sometimes pulling guard IS the absolute best strategy, especially when you're fighting a superior striker who you can't take down. Here are some examples: Rodriguez/Rizzo, Coleman/Fedor, Most Fighters/CroCop, Sherk/St. Pierre, Alessio/Sanchez, Most Fighters/Liddell, etc. etc.

If you master the rubber guard, pulling guard on a fighter that's tattooing you standing and stuffing all your shots will be the most optimal strategy. Now that I think about it, even if you don't master the rubber guard, pulling guard on CroCop will almost always be the best strategy.

...FOR TRUE GLADIATORS!

by Zach Even-Esh

Ages ago warriors and gladiators trained using odd objects and manual labor. Lifting stones and logs, cutting down trees, climbing ropes, and dragging logs or stones attached to rope was a common style of training. These men were strong and extremely tough! Their training promoted strong joints and muscles, reducing injuries. The movements also worked the entire body, creating an efficient form of training. Too many fighters still train like bodybuilders, training specific muscles rather than training movements. Let's take a trip back in time and see what underground training can do for you!

1. Sledge Hammer Training

Strengthens the hands, grip, legs, abdominals and hips. Allows you to use the hammer from overhead and sideways—with both hands or one. Excellent for overall conditioning, improving ground n' pound, as well as improving striking power due to improved hip power! Try doing 10 overhead, 10 left and 10 right. Repeat 4 more times. Build up to doing rounds of 3 to 5 minutes non-stop of 20 to 30 reps in each direction!

2. Sandbag Bent Over Row

An excellent exercise for strengthening your pulling power and grip strength. Hit these hard and heavy if you need to improve your takedowns because your opponent can always sprawl! 4 or 5 heavy sets of 6 to 12 reps will do the trick!

3. Sandbag Shouldering

Getting stuck on your knees at the bottom of your takedowns? Try shouldering a HEAVY sandbag! Squat down and RIP the bag off the ground, onto your shoulder, in one smooth motion. Perform 5 to 6 reps on one shoulder and repeat on the other shoulder for equal reps. Add a shoulder squat at the end of every rep to increase difficulty!

4. Sandbag Squat

Great for strengthening the entire lower body and back. Bear hugging a heavy weight, plus squatting with it, forces the upper and lower body to work harder. Squeeze the bag to work on static strength, improving your clinch game when you need to control your opponent's body. Sink below parallel and do anywhere from 5 to 20 reps. High rep sandbag squats will truly test your mental and physical fortitude!

5. Sandbag Turkish Get Ups

Ever see Chuck Liddell pop off the ground after getting taken down? Crank out this full body exercise with a heavy sandbag. Place the bag on your shoulder, against your chest or try it with arms extended. Perform sets of 5 to 10 reps per set or try doing these "get ups" for 5 minutes non-stop. Get ready to work!

6. Sandbag Whips

Improve your rotational speed through your hips and core. This is great for improving your ability to throw an opponent or resist a throw, as well as improving striking power. The exercise should be done with moderate weights at VERY high speeds. Start low, whip the sandbag up and across, and immediately reverse the action, whipping the bag back down. Repeat for 5 to 10 reps from each side.

SLED TRAINING FOR SKYROCKETING YOUR POWER, STRENGTH & CONDITIONING!

by Zach Even-Esh

If you want a versatile and highly-effective training tool, this may very well be the most important article you've ever read on improving your performance. The sled is a simple training tool that can easily be implemented anywhere outdoors: pavement, grass or sand. Regardless of the surface, sled training works you BIG Time no matter where you are! I personally prefer grass or sand for extra resistance.

Our grapplers use the sled for 10 to 20 minutes non-stop. If you are a highly-competitive grappler and want to test the limits (get the bucket ready), you can go for 30 minutes non-stop (minus quick water sips spread out during the duration of the work out).

The sled is used for lower-body strength development (heavy sled), lower-body endurance (moderate weighted sled) and lower-body power (moderate weighted sled). All movements for the upper body contribute greatly to power because there is no lowering of the weight. You can explode 100 % without worries of controlling the weight on the way down.

All combat athletes need power and speed!

Let's look at a few different sled movements. There are literally over 50 variations one can use with a sled, but these will suffice for now.

FORWARD SLED DRAGS

Most of the time, we walk at a fast pace with the sled. As we reach the end of our dragging distance, we finish with a sprint. Drag for a distance of 150 to 300 feet, then transition to the next movement.

BACKWARD SLED DRAGS

Keeping your shoulder blades retracted (no hunching over), walk backwards for 150 to 300 feet. **This is excellent for lactate tolerance and developing muscular endurance in the lower body!**

ROWING

These can be done with two hands, one hand or as a high pull (squat down and pull hands up above the shoulders). Make sure there is tension on the tow straps and then RIP the handles to your outer rib cage area! Walk back to get tension again and repeat!

PRESSING

Elbows in or out, two hands at a time or one, simply place one foot forward with a slight forward lean, keeping tension on the tow straps and explosively push forward without using the legs. Do not walk forward until the repetition is complete! Alternate the lead foot during each press!

BEAR CRAWL

My absolute favorite full-body sled movement. Perform the bear crawl with the straps attached to a belt. Pull with the hands and drive with the legs!

Here's your ass-kicking sled workout to get you in serious shape fast! Start with 10 minutes non-stop, adding 2 minutes every week until you reach 20 minutes non-stop! Perform this workout 2 times a week!

1A) Forward sled drag x 200 ft., sprint the last 50 ft.
1B) Backward drag x 200 ft., sprint backwards the last 50 ft.
1C) Presses x 6 – 8 reps.
1D) Rowing x 6 – 8 reps.
1E) Bear crawl x 200 ft.
1F) Repeat for prescribed time, NO REST!!!

Zach Even–Esh is a performance coach for combat athletes located in New Jersey. Discover how to skyrocket your performance with your FREE e-book at www.UndergroundCombatTraining.com.

THE BAD ASSES AT THE COUTURE TRAINING CENTER

RANDY "THE NINJA" COUTURE

SVEN BEAN, FREDDY, RJ, AND JOKER AT A RADIO SHOW IN DENVER

DUANE LUDWIG SHOWING OFF HIS SEXY SLEEP WEAR

38 FOOT RV + 17 FOOT TRAILER + ROCKY MOUNTAIN BLIZZARD = HELL OF A LOT OF FUN

WES SIMS

JOKER GOING FOR A RIDE AT CAESAR'S PALACE

ED SOARES AND KEVIN RANDLEMAN

I THINK THEY LIKE THE RV

MIKE PYLE SMELLING HIS "FEET"

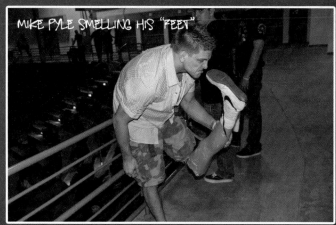

KRAZY HORSE, JAMES LEE, AND THE BEAUTIFUL KOTC RING GIRLS

PARKED IN FRONT OF THE LEGENDARY LA FORUM FOR THE IFL

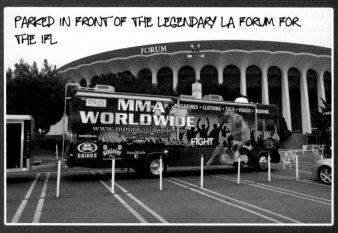

BOBBY, FREDDY, AND MAURICE SMITH

RAMPAGE TAKING CONTROL OF THE INTERVIEW

TRAVIS LUTTER AND RJ

FREDDY, NICK DIAZ, AND RJ AT THE BOOTH

Little League

Brother Sean, Chuck, and Sister Laura

Laura, Chuck, and Sean

In the last issue of **MMA Worldwide**, our cover story on Chuck Liddell included pictures of him growing up and life outside the cage. Thanks to Chuck's sister Laura, we have more photos than we could possibly use for one cover story. With these photos too priceless to leave on the drawing board (and to Chuck's dismay), the collage for this issue of **MMA Worldwide** will be all of Chuck's early years.

Sadie Hawkins Dance, Chuck's first date (He forgot his wallet!)

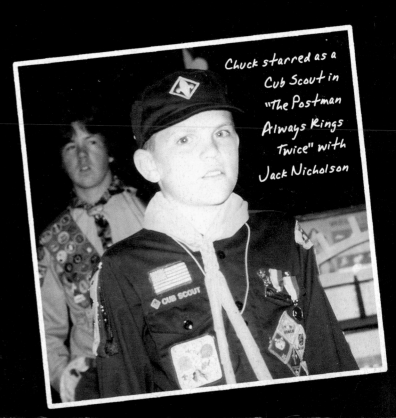

Chuck starred as a Cub Scout in "The Postman Always Rings Twice" with Jack Nicholson

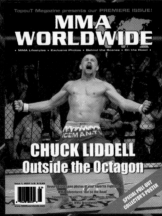